CLIMBING OUT OF DEBT

Practical steps to manage your money, take away from
fear and put you back in control

NICK STURGEON

Bridgewater Ink

Published by Bridgewater Ink Limited

Introduction

Debt Free, and Loving it!

I have struggled for years with debt at different times of my life.

Until I went to college debt was never an issue because I worked if I wanted money, and rested when I considered that I had enough money. I was unaware of credit or borrowing because No one had ever offered me a bank loan and I had yet to know about credit cards or store cards. Every time I needed more cash I would find an extra job. Sometimes I would earn money by trading things that I liked to handle, buying them from one person and selling them to another. For a year after school I enjoyed good money buying vintage military memorabilia and old equipment in my home town at markets and stalls, taking it down to London by train once a month and selling for good profits. I loved the game involved in buying at a low price and selling for a higher one, and in finding the sources for the purchases and then looking at who would want the products I needed to dispose of. I never needed to borrow and all the trades were for cash.

However, leaving home to spend several years studying at college was a real tough introduction to borrowing money. To begin with the bank offered me a loan for the first year of moving to the city in case I needed it to be available. Did I need it? No, but I certainly made sure I spent enough money for that loan to be useful and also for it to be used up completely!

When I graduated from college I found myself with a beautiful degree certificate to hang on the wall. It officially confirmed that I knew lots of 'stuff' about my specialist topic. It did not say that I had accumulated a far less impressive and much more painful student debt of more than $3,000 pounds. For the first year of work this debt haunted me and simply got larger one month and back again to three thousand the next month. Why was this the case? Because I would earn my salary, have it paid into the bank and see my loan reduced only to then see that the cost of living my own life each month pushed the debt back up again over the next 30 days or so, leaving me right back at the beginning of the debt cycle. One step forward and one step back.

No matter what I did for that first year, I was simply riding on top of a cushion of debt that expanded and stretched each month, never going away.

That was my first year of working. When I received a promotion and much better pay the following year I had expected that my debt would become manageable, that I could get in control of it because of the higher income. Is this what happened? You know it isn't! My debt got worse because my expenditure had risen to match the new income. Watch out for this one!

On a higher salary I was actually worse off. So much so that at the end of year two, and even though I was earning almost $8,000 more a year in the new job, my debt had gone from that familiar level of $3,000 and increased to $7,000.

So now I was two years out of college with a $7,000 debt. My debt had more than doubled in just twelve months for two clear reasons:

I was earning more and had increased my spending accordingly, but

I had actually reduced the percentage of my earnings that was going to debt reduction.

All the time I was running up more credit card commitments and only paying the minimum on them whilst seeing high rates of interest being applied to the unpaid amounts each month.

Fast forward another ten years and I was in a place where I had left employed work and by then been self-employed for five years. I was working with new business start-ups, helping them to develop business plans, create and understand cash-flow forecasts and connect with the relationship between pricing, trading figures and profits for their ventures. Yet, I was still carrying a fairly standard $3,000 of personal debt from one month to the next. It is almost as if I was comfortable with it, unconcerned that I was living with an overdraft facility at the bank.

No matter what I earned, I was stuck in the cycle of

debt, unable to escape or to claw my way out of it. Stuck until I had a chance meeting with a friend who could see the struggle I was going through and introduced me to some of the concepts I am sharing with you in this book.

Move ahead another ten years and to all the learning and financial adventures that I was fortunate enough to have by creating my own businesses. I had been building capital, creating a property portfolio, making lots of money, and connecting with and learning from other helpful people who each shared with me a part of their own knowledge. I was financially strong and had a great lifestyle. We employed half a dozen people and enjoyed what we had created with the portfolio of houses we had created together.

Move forward another decade and I lost the property portfolio that had taken me years to build up, and which I had enjoyed tremendously. But the fall and the learning from this allowed me to start working again with small business owners and people who had struggled with their finances and not been able to escape from debt. I showed them how to keep their creditors under control, helped them to pay down debt, increase their incomes, start to save percentages of their earnings and pay their bills on time, just as I had learned to. In the process I have been able to start acquiring and refurbishing properties again and to develop good commercial income on these.

So if you are having doubts about if you can weather the storm, get rid of them now. Between the pages of this book are some of the answers you need.

My intention is that as you find the guidance and information that will help you to get back in control of your debt paperwork, to build up your finances and put cash in the bank. You will develop the peace of mind that comes from knowing that your money is working for you.

Nick

Yorkshire, England

ONE

Welcome to recovery!

IN LOOKING for a new role after saying goodbye to my work as a property owning landlord, I was invited to join a social enterprise organization. They provided debt guidance and money advice to people seeking support and a way forward. I loved the work and it was a place where I could use my own life experience on both sides of the 'money fence.'

MONEY MATTERS - NIGEL & Kate.

Every day at the Money Advice Centre would bring new surprises. I clearly remember starting an appointment with a young couple who came to see us. Nigel and Kate were just in their late twenties and with three young children, one of whom was crawling around the meeting room and crayoning happily on the clean white walls! His parents seemed oblivious of this. Up to their necks in debt and scared of drowning in it, they had long since lost the ability to focus on everything going on around them. I was used to this and had seen it many times, but I want to share their debt story with you as an example.

Nigel and Kate had turned up for this second meeting with a carrier bag of unopened post, a wad of crumpled financial statements and a lot of 'fears and tears' on display. How had it got to this stage? How could a lovely young couple, clearly devoted to each other and their children, manage to find themselves in such a mess and seeking help from the debt guidance team in their local town?

I'll tell you how they got here, and you can see immediately that this is how any of us can get into trouble with money. Nine years before, at a young age they were newly married and managed to find a very low deposit mortgage, meaning they borrowed 95% from a willing bank and 5% on a credit card and found themselves the happy owners of a brand new two bedroom house. For three years they had paid the minimum on their credit card and seen the balance balloon to twice the original amount they borrowed, going into default on the debt, losing the credit card, and paying fixed amounts each month to another company that had bought the debt from the original credit card issuer. How much had they paid? How much were they paying? They had no idea. What did they owe?

As debt increases and pressure on household income is raised, the ability to notice debt can go out the window. In addition to the credit card debt, they were in arrears on three store card accounts. Two mail order catalogue distributors were also writing each month for a minimum payment, but not always receiving it from Nigel and Kate. The debts were growing disproportionately to the original loans. Yes, much of this was due to lack of action or attention, but also for the absence of understanding.

Towards the bottom of the bag were some more envelopes they had not opened! Big, white and official looking document envelopes. These were from the mortgage company, with some other more recent ones from the solicitors for the mortgage company not just threatening legal action, but actually issuing dates for court action and a potential repossession hearing. Also, within the bag were a few envelopes from another creditor seeking a response from Nigel and Kate. These related to a second charge, where they had borrowed money and had given the lender of the small loan some security in the form of a charge (more correctly called a Charging Order) on their house! Positioned behind the mortgage company, this second lender potentially had the power to seek a forced sale of the house in the event of non-payment. Things were bad, potentially catastrophic. Our role was to point out the facts of the situation and look at what actions they could take in response.

The old credit card debt was now $9,000. The store cards and catalogue debt came to a total of $2,300. The mortgage arrears were $7,800 out of a total mortgage debt of $74,000 and the lender had requested a court date for a hearing before a district judge to discuss a repossession action and the eviction of the family.

In summary:
Debt
Monthly Payment

CREDIT CARD

$ 9,000

$ 500

Store Cards

$ 2,300

$ 160

Mortgage Arrears

$ 7,800

$ 190

Secured Debt

$ 6,000

$ 230

Totals

$25,100

$1,080

THE NEED TO find $1,080 a month to fund these minimum commitments might not seem bad especially when you consider that two of these monthly bills – for the mortgage and the secured charge total just $420 as the cost for living in their house. But of course, the $1,080 represents just the minimum payments and so the overall debt continues to increase each month.

Now for the really bad news! Kate had stopped work the year before due to her stress and panic attacks which prevented her from turning up regularly at work. Nigel had finished work two months ago after a dispute over pay with his former employer – possibly where the small firm he worked for needed to cut their own staff numbers and save costs – but which had been dealt with in a poor and unprofessional manner. He was registered to start up in business on his own, but it would be another two months before he would qualify for the government endorsed and supported start-up scheme and the associated weekly contribution to replace his unemployed status benefit monies. They seemed to be stuck between a rock and a hard place.

So from a welfare benefits income of around $700 a month, they were of course struggling to find $1,080 on top of what they required to pay for food, heating, clothes and nappies for the children and to run their one low value car.

WHAT HAPPENED **to Nigel and Kate?**

After this second meeting we, as the Money Advice Centre, were in touch with the solicitors for the lender and with the second charge holder. We waited until they issued a Court date for a formal Hearing with a District Judge and I attended that Hearing with Nigel and Kate, effectively representing them in the scary world (if it is your first time) of going to such a meeting. In reality it was simply the District Judge, a solicitor for the lender and the three of us in a small meeting room. The Judge listened thoughtfully to the requirements of the lender for possession. A date was sought by the lender for one month ahead and which we (the debt advice center) contested by asking for a longer forward date. We asked for this in order to give us time to find alternative accommodation within the private rented sector i.e. with a private landlord in the same town. The Judge agreed to this request and we left the Court with two months to sort the new accommodation out.

Within three weeks of our debt support session Nigel and Kate had found a new rental property to move into. They registered with the social housing team in order to apply for housing benefit income at a level that matched the new house they needed as a family and Nigel was beginning to start providing quotes and estimates for customers of his soon-to-start business. After trying to find a buyer for the house and having several wasted meetings with investors who wanted the mortgage only arrangement on the house and did not want to deal with the second charge debt, they eventually met with a land-lord who agreed to buy the property for the value of the two combined house debts. He struck a deal with the mortgage company to take over their mortgage and with the second charge lender to repay the $6,000.

Nigel and Kate were then able to structure a Debt Relief Order (DRO) that wrapped up the credit card debt and also the debts for the store cards and cata-logues. This arrangement cost them around $100 and allowed them to write-off the $11,300 in one process.

Another month further on, and by now settled well in their new rented property, Nigel was earning steady income from his new business. They were working together well as a couple, the focus on raising their three children and having agreed not to repeat their debt behaviors again.

IT'S NOT ALL **about You!**

I share the story of this couple so that you can see early on the common mistakes we can all very easily make, and which lead us into difficult debt. Right now, you may feel that this is your problem and your problem alone. This is completely understandable and when I had the heaviest of my own debt problems, I actually made them worse by not discussing either the size of the financial problem or my own fears with others. Debt challenges can often become much more manageable when you discuss the issue with other people. So, stop thinking this is just about you. A problem shared really is a problem halved. Get used to talking about your debt. I don't mean get used to complaining about the debt. Instead, talk openly about your money worries with people who can help you with the combined aspects of Advice, Guidance and some Moral Support. Not one of these, but all three.

These days most towns will have at least one office or community forum where you can book an appointment and get help with the issues. Trying to tough it out, or face the problem on your own, is a real mistake. Get help and get it now. Your local authority will have a dedicated team of people whose main activity every day is talking to and working with individuals and families who are struggling in debt and worried sick with fear and stress. One family in debt has little impact on the economy of a town. Many households in debt affects the whole community and so it becomes an important issue that needs to be addressed, dealt with and supported.

Debt is one of the most significant causes of relationship breakdown. It adds hugely to personal mental health issues and in a very negative way. If you are unable to sleep for worry of debt, scared of who might be knocking at your front door to collect an unpaid bill, or of the post arriving through your mailbox, then you need to seek help. Start today!

GET OVER YOURSELF!

So, you're in debt? Join the club. This is not a club that promotes the benefits of membership or invites other people to join. It is a secret place where people sit on their own, sucking their thumbs or crying into their coffee, waiting for something to change. It is a club where the hard-luck story is the dominant one, where we might imagine that our own situation is worse than another person's. But hear this, it is not a place to stay, it is not a place to tell people about and do nothing.

To get out of debt requires steady action every day. I can't promise you when you will be out of debt as the amount you owe will be different from the debt of your neighbor or a work colleague or someone within your study group. Most of the time we each suffer in silence with debt, making a bad job of dealing with it. Debt is easy to pile on. It requires work and effort to get rid of.

I can tell you now that no amount of worrying about your debt, or your feelings about having it, is going to make it go away. But I will show you within these pages plenty of ways that you can define it, start to tackle it and then to begin the process of paying it off. The moment you can define it and measure it, your debt ceases to be in control of you and you have the chance to take back the reins for yourself. Climbing out of debt is a great achievement.

HOW WE GET INTO DEBT.

It can be the simplest thing. We might be late into work one day and have to take a taxi because there is no public transport. We borrow $20 for the taxi from a neighbor or family member and promise to repay it next week on payday. But we forget to pay it back or we pay late.

We are driving in the car and get a flat tire from an old nail that causes the puncture. So, we pull over at the garage and get the tire replaced. This costs $50 for the tire and another $30 for the labor involved in fitting it. So, we pull out the credit card and charge the new $80 debt to the finance company, with the full understanding that we will cover it at the end of the month when the bill is due to be settled.

You are in town for shopping and some window browsing. A new shirt in the window of the clothing store just calls out to you, and you have to go in and take a look at it. You know you are not going to buy it, as it costs $35 because it looks so good. You justify the cost of this against the potential benefits. Your partner will certainly think you look more gorgeous in it, your employer will consider you a better candidate for the next round of employee promotions, and you could even wear it casually for a party. And so, the excuses come into your head until you walk out of the shop with it charged to your debit card and the money gone forever from your bank account.

WHAT YOU WANT versus what you Need.

Here are some painful truths to deal with and face up to:

You wanted to get the taxi to avoid being late for work. Yet you could have set your alarm, got up on time and have used your transport card which already gives you good value access to the bus and the metro system in your town.

You needed the new car tire because that really is a genuine expenditure you had to cover. Your car gets you out and around the area, and it serves as good transport for the family.

The shirt you wanted but did not need. You have enough existing clothes in your home wardrobe that you could wear a different shirt every day for 3 weeks and all of them are quite good enough for your partner, for a work meeting or for a dinner with friends. You wanted it, you had no self-control and you wasted $35 that should have stayed in your account. You acted impulsively when you had no plan for spending on your wardrobe.

· · ·

YOU ARE NOT ALONE.

Millions of us struggle with debt from day to day. Whether you live on your own, in a partnership or with a spouse and family to support, debt is no more a stranger to one of these household types than another.

Debt doesn't care who wants to encourage it, extend it, hang on to it or suffer with it. It takes no sides and it takes all sides. Debt clings on aggressively where it finds an easy foothold. It sticks hard to any environment where things are slack, chaotic or poorly managed. Debt is your enemy.

Debt can destroy friendships and crush previously good relationships by placing itself at the forefront of worries, discussions and arguments. It can be the cause of divorce, secrecy, stealth and avoidance of truth. But only if you let it.

And this experience is one that all of us have now or have known at some point in our lives. The core issue to remember is that it is not just you. Regardless of whether you live in a street of twenty houses or of two hundred houses, you can be sure that a large number of these have known some struggle with debt, with poor money management, with not enough money at the end of the month. Whatever term or phrase you choose, it is enough to describe not having enough money to pay all the bills. Debt really is everywhere.

Debt cuts across all social groupings and levels of earnings. Whether you earn $100,000 a year or $20,000 a year the impact of debt is the same. You don't have enough money for your expenditure needs, and you must do something about it. You have debt and must deal with it. Debt is debt. Whether you owe $1,000 or you owe $10,000 is close to irrelevant if the amount you owe is greater than your ability to repay it. You are still unable to afford that amount. It really matters only very little what the figure is. There simply comes a moment where our debt impacts our lives negatively. You need to recognize that moment when it arrives and acknowledge that you are willing to something about it.

WHAT DEBT DOES TO YOU.

Opening a letter from a utility company to find a higher bill than you are expecting can have a dreadful impact on you. It might make your throat go dry, cause your heart to race, or make you feel weak at the knees for fear of being unable to pay it.

Receiving a medical bill or an insurance charge for something that you needed, but which you put onto a credit payment arrangement, can have such an impact on you as to instantly remove any of the good that came from the procedure, the treatment or the remedial work that was so necessary at the time of purchase.

Hiding a debt from a partner will cause you to behave out of character, to lie or to pretend that things are well, while all the time the dark presence of the debt is draining you of energy, of vitality and of being your real self.

Each letter or unidentified call to your mobile phone, is another source of anxiety and of fear taking a grip on you. The shame and pain of carrying secret debt can manifest into high blood pressure, anxiety, depression and even thoughts of a suicidal nature. It can rob you of sleep, of good health, and of personal happiness for the sake of carrying with you the worries, the fears and the torment of being out of control with our finances. Being in debt is painful and unpleasant.

It is also completely unnecessary. Yes, you don't need to live like this or to put up with ongoing debt. You have the chance to fight back and to begin - slowly and steadily at first - to take back control of your money matters.

SEE BEYOND THE BILLS.

There is a future place for you where you will have no debt. Think about this for a minute.

"There is a place where you will have no debt."

In that place you will be so proud of yourself for what you have accomplished and for the journey you have made to reach the place of being debt free.

This is a place where - before you open them - you know already the content of the letters from your energy suppliers, from your house lender, from your car dealer, from your insurance company. These letters are simply telling you that your account is settled, that your balance is just what you expect to be. Such letters are simply confirming what you know - that you have no unwanted debt.

WHAT WILL 'SORTED' **feel like?**

Being debt free is a good place to be. It is the place

to aim for and to set as your personal target destination. Knowing that there are no financial surprises will give you peace of mind.

There will always be an unexpected car bill, or some household maintenance that comes with a change in seasons. There will sometimes be accidental damage. However, knowing that you have money available for such things means that they do not shock you and they absolutely cannot hurt you.

Take a moment to reflect on how you felt when you were not struggling with debt and the thoughts you had then. Can you recall situations where you coped well with your finances and the management of your money? Consider what these situations were like and the feeling you had of being in control, of having your finances in order. Any time you feel panic or worry about your financial circumstances, try to recall the times when all was ok and to know that you can get yourself back to that place. It is going to take some work, some diligence, the application of some new habits and the will to be debt free.

LEARNING POINTS.

> A problem can be simplified when you give your attention to it.

> Facing the problem on your own is a mistake.

> Getting out of debt requires daily action.

> Other people are in debt too.

> Fight back and take control.

> It will take work and you can be debt free.

TWO

Watch out for the warning signs

IT MIGHT HAVE COME as a slow realization that you
are in debt, but if you are honest with yourself then it
can't actually have come as a shock. If you look at how
you got to this place, there were various warnings signs
along the way. These little indicators don't seem to indi-
vidually trouble you or call your full attention until the
volume of them becomes the real problem.

UNOPENED Mail

For me, and for the households that I have worked
with, the first sign is the stacks of envelopes placed
around the house. You can seem them on dining tables,
on a shelf in the hallway, stuffed against the arm of a
sofa. Perhaps they are bundled with an elastic band and
pushed between some food jars in the kitchen or hidden
between the wall and the microwave. Every pile, stack or
bundle is the same. They are still unopened envelopes.
Maybe you are not the sort of person who lets these

things be seen. You hide them, you don't let them be on display. You keep these tell-tale signs of your troubles out of sight of visitors. That's if you even let people into your space at all. You might fill a dark drawer with the post, or stuff them in a carrier bag.

MONEY MATTERS - MELANIE **& Peter.**

Melanie and Peter, a married couple in their forties and with two teenage children, presented me with four carrier bags of unopened post when I saw them as clients at the Money Advice Centre. The fear in their eyes at actually handing over these bags, at letting a stranger see the extent of their indebtedness, this fear was something I could almost touch in the air between us. After they had left the office it took me three hours to open the post, to sort out the different creditor demands and to then file the latest statements into a binder. Their total debt figure was $14,500 of monies owed.

Not opening the post, not dealing with the issue of the debt is a lot like sticking your head in the sand, in adopting the ostrich pose and imagining that No one can see the mess. The problem with this behavior, apart from the obvious issue that it stops you knowing the extent of your situation, is that it means you don't open a single thing that looks official.

MONEY MATTERS - MANDY.

Mandy, a grandmother I visited in her house because she didn't want to be seen walking into our offices by any of her friends in town, brought her unopened post to the kitchen table and we spent an hour sifting through it together. Within the envelopes was one credit note from her own local authority tax office, returning the actual amount of $202 she had overpaid. A second envelope contained a refund cheque of $47 on car insurance. She had reached another birthday, but not wised up to the fact that she was eligible for cheaper car insurance. So, open your post. You can't resolve a problem that is not defined. Neither can you find a solution to something when you don't fully know the extent of it.

AN UNMONITORED AND UNBALANCED ACCOUNT.

You still issue checks, set up regular monthly bank orders and debit arrangements, but you are amazed when one fails or bounces or simply does not get paid. In your mind ignorance is bliss and you are comforted falsely into thinking that it is best to not know. You think you've enough money for the full week ahead, but you're not really sure.

DELAYING PAYING.

Your website developer has issued you with an invoice for their work. Your bookkeeper has sent you an email telling you the amount that you owe for the work she has done to get your accounts in order to get you to a place where – because of her work – you will have an accurate figure for your likely tax bill this year. Your landlord has sent you a reminder of your rent payment date, along with a letter that provides the details of her switch to a new business bank account.

You figure that you can send just half of the agreed figure to your web developer. You delay the money to your bookkeeper another week and claim to have been too busy to make the payment. You don't pay the rent until the landlord chases you with a polite SMS message asking when you paid the rent and tells you she is trying to match your credit against others she has in her account this week. You reply with a message that you didn't get the new bank details and will send straightaway.

With this attitude you've lost the confidence of your website developer and also of the person you really need to help keep your tax bill down. You've tricked your landlord out of prompt payment for your accommodation and you think you've done yourself a favor. But now it's only three weeks until the next month's rent is due. You've only fooled yourself.

PAYING FOR YOUR BANK ACCOUNT.

You pay a monthly amount of $10 or $20 to your bank and you allow them to take this from your account in exchange for points that are supposed to add up to something exciting like a discount on shopping at stores you don't frequently use, or that gives you reduced entry tickets to a theme park you will never visit. You do this, you allow them to charge for such a "privilege" account, but at the same time you have debts that are greater than the amount of $120 or $240 you are handing over each year.

Similar to the bank account, you might have a membership of a VIP Dining Card scheme that you pay a monthly fee for, and yet you either don't use the card enough for it to be a worthwhile membership or you go out to such meals and sit there sweating at the prospect of the bill after the meal being more than you know you should be spending. If you are uncomfortable then stop kidding yourself that this is a real or relevant thing in your life. Get your money in order and enjoy a meal as a reward for sorting things out.

IT'S NOT **the 1st of the month again, is it?**

You open your online banking account secretly hoping that there is $500 in your account and are disappointed or even angry when you see that you have just $180 available now that the water, electric and gas monies have been taken out, along with the grocery store money and the petrol from the weekend. You are a week from getting your next wage credit to your account and you know you will struggle to get through these next days. The chemist will need to be paid $37 for your prescription drugs today. Your car really does need two new front tires at $60 each tire, and the weather is not good. There is a $29 school meal invoice to be paid. You complain that life is not fair to you! Everyone else has it so much easier than you!

Get this into your head. *It is irrelevant where other people are with their money.* It is pointless thinking about anything other than what you can start to do differently or better around the way that you deal with your money.

THIS IS JUST TOO COMPLICATED!

It's the role of someone else to help you. You can't manage your money on your own. You need to find help, but you don't know where to turn and you can't be bothered to make it a priority to go out and find a solution to the problems you are expressing.

"I can't be expected to balance my accounts on my own."

"It's OK for them. They are better educated and understand this stuff better than me."

"She can manage her money. She's more savvy than I am."

"I can't do this number stuff. I did bad at mathematics when I was at school."

"My own expenses are so different from my neighbor / workmate / brother ..."

"I could do this if only my parents had explained all this to me when I was a kid."

"It's difficult for me on my low income in this job."

These are just a few of the reasons I have heard people give for being out of control when it comes to money. It doesn't matter what the reason is that they give. The one that you like to use or have latched on to when explaining your difficulties around money is just an excuse. It is an excuse for pushing the responsibility away and either giving it to someone else who should have helped you or taught you or shown you how to do this *"money stuff."* They didn't. So, get over it.

ANY OF THESE items are the warning signs of your debting behavior. When it comes to sorting out your debts and dealing with your money in a way that works, then you have to recognize that you need to let go of the excuses. Only you know your numbers. Only you can make the changes in the way that you deal with money in your life.

We all deal with money differently. None of us are the same. My experience of debt is unique to me. Yours is personal to you.

If you see yourself in any one or more of the warning signs then it's time to start to adopt a few new habits. There is a quote that says :

> *"The definition of madness is doing the same thing*
> *again and again while expecting a different result."*

I like the truth of the words. If you are doing the same things with your money month after month - and you are still unable to pay all your bills – then something needs to change this month if you are going to make positive progress. You are what needs to change. You have created the situation you are in by the small actions and consistent behaviors you have made to reach this miserable place. The lack of control, the fear, the embarrassment, each of these feelings is real. The good news though, is that you have all the resources you need to become debt free and the first step along the way is to recognize that the mistakes have been made.

If you are continuing to ignore the post, telephone calls from creditors, and are still experiencing the fear of a 'decline' message when you tap or swipe your bank card in a shop or café, then let's start to do some things differently.

You don't want to continue your debting.

We all want to deny that the problem is here, or to pretend that we are not affected by debt. This is natural behavior to protect ourselves, to defend against the suggestion that we are out of control financially. Going forward from here, your solutions lie in changing your debting behavior and adopting new practices around money. Not just about earning money, though increasing your income is an important place to focus your attention. At the same time you need to recognize the need to change the way you shop, adapt the current poor saving behavior, and to cut your costs in every single place you can.

YOU DON'T HAVE **to be In Debt.**

Your debts are unnecessary, and you can let go of them. You can stop them from crushing you, from beating you down each day. Yes, they are a problem and one that you can solve. You can eliminate the problem if you follow a simple set of steps to get you back into a place of control, a place where you can pay your bills and put the debt fear behind you. Admit now that you have a debting problem and let's make some lasting changes together.

LEARNING POINTS.

> Don't kid yourself that you want something unnecessary.

> Paying something on time is better than paying nothing late.

> It doesn't matter how other people deal with money.

> Stop using excuses to justify your debting situation.

> We all deal with money differently.

> It's your own behavior around money that needs to change.

> You don't want to continue your debting.

> The solutions are in adopting new practices around money.

> Cut your costs everywhere you can.

THREE

Different thinking for different results

YOU GOT yourself into debting habits through thinking that clearly wasn't right for you, so maybe we need to take a new approach. Recognizing and accepting the truth of this – that you are approaching money with the wrong mindset – is the starting point for getting in control of your money. You can get yourself out of this.

There's nothing soft headed about the approaches offered to you here. They are all tried and tested with many people who have made this journey from debt to no debt, from stress and worry to having a cash surplus in the bank. Your resistance to the change, to trying out new things that actually work is completely to be expected after years of you following patterns of money behavior that have not served you or supported you.

YOU ARE OK TODAY. Yes, really!
Right now, you have enough to live through the

whole day. You have clothes on and can access enough food to eat. You have a place to sleep this evening. You have the desire to get out of debt and you know that you want so much to make things different. Knowing that you have what you need for survival right now allows you to see that – if you start to make changes to your behavior around money and with money – that you can create new results in your life.

You are safe right now. You are not required to spend money on things that you do not need, to impress people you do not like or to get into any more debt over something that you do not want to do.

Sit calmly for a moment and look around you. You are OK. You have all that you need to get through today. Perhaps you are at home and reading this on a laptop or a tablet device. Maybe you are in a library or sneaking a peak in a bookstore. Are you in a coffee shop just like me as I write this? You have clothes on your back. You have enjoyed a breakfast or a lunch. You know where you will be this afternoon and roughly what your evening is looking like.

Maybe yesterday really was dreadful. But it's over and done with. It's not coming back to get you, so just let it go. Tomorrow's not here yet, so don't waste time worrying about what it might bring. You are in today only. Right now, you are only in this moment. As you go through today, reflect on this. Repeat the exercise of thinking about what you have. Keep your focus on what you have.

For example, I am in the upstairs room of my local

independent coffee shop. On the wooden trestle table in front of me I have a supply of clean, unlined paper. I have a nice pen and a couple of spares. A large cappuccino is by my side, in a takeaway cup with a lid on it to keep it warm while I write. I am listening to some cheerful music direct from my phone and through my headphones. I am wearing clean clothes and have some coins in my pocket to get a sandwich when I am ready. I am ok. I am safe. I am in this moment only.

WHERE ARE YOU RIGHT NOW?

You can step out of the moment if you want to. But don't project yourself into another day, into a place that is busy with piles of debts and unopened post. Doing that will not serve you if it causes you to feel stressed, to be anxious, to try and struggle for a solution that takes up yet more energy. None of that is real. It will not help or support you in any good way so let go of it. Focus instead on where you are now. In this moment, right now, you have all that you need to be who you are. You are ok and you are safe. You have all that you need.

YOUR DEBT IS TEMPORARY.

You are not your debt. You are the color of your eyes. You are your height and your experience of life so far. But in the same way that you are not your job because you are capable of doing it and also of doing something else, you are not your debt. Your debt is a temporary situation and you are able to change this for a different situation, one that is more appealing, more attractive to you and less stressful. How do you make the change from having debt - from being out of control with your money - to somewhere better?

The answer is really simple. You are not going to take on another Pound, Dollar or Euro of debt. You are going to pay back each of the people or organizations that you owe money to and you are going to pay them in full. The thing to focus on is that you are going to do this one pound, one dollar or one euro at a time, and only in a way that allows you to do so while enjoying your own life each day. From this point on you are going to pay down your debt one unit of money at a time.

MONEY MATTERS - BUSINESS **owner pays back $22,500.**

Susan ran a PR and Marketing business from a spare room in her beautiful farmhouse. When I first met her there almost five years ago, she had debt of $27,000. These were the combined cost of some mistakes she had made in business and the price of some lifestyle changes. She was at the point of giving up on life. She was close to losing her home with three mortgage payments unmade and a lot of correspondence from her lender that she was ignoring. We spent several hours looking at her debts and her income. She was invoicing clients promptly, but only chased them slowly. She was also missing out on various potential opportunities for increasing her income.

. . .

FAST FORWARD TO today and she has reduced her debt to $4,500. Her lovely home is paid for each month with no delays to her mortgage lender and no arrears owed. Her business operates profitably, and she is in regular contact with her creditors by letter every three months with a written financial statement. Susan is enjoying her life and the operation of her business. She is happy with her situation and pleased with the simple changes she has made to the way that she handles her money.

MONEY MATTERS - Young family clear $10,000 of debt.

Almost two years ago a couple came to see me at the Money Advice Centre. Arthur worked nights in a factory and Yvette worked part-time as a school administrator in their local neighborhood. They were young parents to 3 children. They carried debt of $18,000 which was about 6 months of their combined work income. They had struggled with creditors, ignored a lot of correspondence, borrowed at extortionate rates from payday loan companies and were at their wits end emotionally from the constant stress and strain of not dealing with their debts. They had been fighting with each other frequently, arguing about the problems and had lost sight of any workable solution. They feared that the stress would break them as a couple and were worried about the children hearing them argue so often.

Now things are more straightforward, and they are in control of the situation. Their numbers are far better with $10,000 gone and $8,000 left to pay down. Theirs is no longer the struggle that it was the first time we met. All their papers and correspondence fit into one ring binder and there are no surprises waiting to catch them out. They have enjoyed a foreign holiday that they paid for from their intentionally created holiday savings account with no borrowing involved. They are happier and more comfortable together than they have been for several years. They are communicating well, and they are happy.

YOU HAVE THE SOLUTION.

No one else is going to help you escape from your debt. Susan is not going to be your financial savior. Arthur and Yvette will not be coming to your rescue. You don't need them, and you don't need anyone else to get out of this. You are your own solution.

You can apply the actions, recommendations and concepts outlined here to get yourself out of debt one unit of money at a time. You can join many others who have already done this, and you can put yourself in a new position of financial confidence and of comfort. It starts now.

LEARNING POINTS.

> You can get yourself out of this.

> You have enough to get through the whole day.
> You are not your debts.
> Yesterday is over and done with.
> You have the solution.

FOUR

Be yourself

JUST BE YOURSELF.

This book is written for **you**. It is not for the people you have borrowed from. You may be a student, a retiree, a person in work or on benefit street. You might be receiving just state or government payments as your only income. You may be single. You could be secretly in debt without your partner being aware. You might have one main job and a part-time job alongside. You might be a networker with a social referral business and some great product. Maybe you are a couple facing your debts together, supporting each other in the process. You are a friend, a partner, a companion, a supporter, and a member of your community. I want you to just be yourself.

Your sense of excitement about life is directly affected by the amount of time you spend doing the things and the hobbies that you love. Your experiences have given you insight into what is important for you, into how you value some things over others, into how you make decisions that help you feel happier, more fulfilled, and which allow you to know what is right for you.

You have friends, family and social networks that you are part of. You are valuable and important to all these people. They want the best for you in terms of happiness, fun, joy, compassion and self-worth.

You will love music, words, poetry or film. Your senses are stirred by touch, hunger, sound, warmth and intimacy.

Who are you then? You are all these suggested ideas, thoughts and imaginings captured here in a few moments of writing. All these things and much more are you.

Are you $12,000 of debts and a car as an asset worth $7,000? No.

Are you $23,200 of debts and a house worth $100,000 more than the mortgage loan value? No.

Are you $6,470 of debts and no savings and a weekly paid job? No.

You are not the debt. The debt is not you. You are not defined by your debt.

Do not fall into a place where you let yourself be defined by your debt. Do not even allow anyone to judge you by the existence of your debts or by the value of them. You are still not your debts. You are all the good, rich, valuable, deep and genuine experiences that have made you who you are.

. . .

YOU ARE a Free Agent in all of this.

You are not the property of the DIY store that you owe $400 to for supplies that you still have not paid for. The bank that loaned you money for a car (that you no longer have, and which has $1,200 still due to be repaid), that bank does not own you.

Neither are you the property of the credit card company. They approached you in a mailing campaign and you signed up for a $500 Credit Improver Card. You've never managed to pay it off and still owe them $460 even though you have been paying more than the minimum amount each month for more than two years and you stopped buying anything with it eighteen months ago.

As a debtor it is easy to fall into the trap of becoming obsessively aware of the debts. You let them haunt you. They rob you of vitality, of spontaneity, of living in the moment. But you are not owned by your debts, so don't be controlled by them. Don't allow them to dominate every aspect of your life. Be yourself. You are absolutely NOT YOUR DEBTS.

You've already looked at and understood the principle that your debts are temporary. Now it's time to understand and accept the fact that your creditors do own the debt that you owe them, and they do own the right to communicate with you about making payment.

YOUR CREDITORS DO NOT OWN You.

To get out of your debt situation your main point of

focus must be yourself. You are not responsible for the creditors, only for your response to dealing with the debt.

You deserve to enjoy your life. Claim it as yours. It may be true that in this month or for several years while you have been facing and attempting to deal with the letters, calls, emails and doorstep visits from the people and the organizations you owe money to, that you have lost the focus on yourself. It is completely understandable that you have taken your eyes off the prize, away from the right you have to put yourself first, to do the things that make you who you truly are when at your happiest and most fulfilled. Stop being a prisoner to your debt.

Grab control of your own life. Grasp it with both hands and take it back for yourself. Live for yourself again. Fill your days and your weeks with the activities that are important and meaningful to you.

Strengths that will come to you from making this decision to get back on track will bring about great positive changes. This is not hocus-pocus. It is not light-headed thinking. Focus on you and you will see good improvements to your thinking, to your well-being, and very likely to the ability to influence your money and the opportunities that come to you. The more you grow into yourself, the faster you will be able to deal with your debts and move to that point where they are reducing until finally paid off.

OPEN Your Eyes to What You Have.

Too long seemingly surrounded by your bills, by your debts and all the associated fears can close down your own sense of proportion to your total life picture. It's as though the debt has put a gray lens over your eyes so that you can't recognize all the good stuff around you. You don't see all the amazing things, the kind people, the caring friends and the opportunities that are being offered to you.

A couple of years after my divorce I was having a beer with my old friend Paul. We had known each other ever since we met during our university days when we had both lived and studied in Mexico. We had caught up again after perhaps five years. We had gone to a small-town pub, one with a log fire in the bar, a great menu described intelligently on a large chalk board, a book-borrow section, and friendly staff. My ideal place! He was telling me about a recent trip back to Mexico, describing the coastal town where he had studied, how he had met his wife and how things were going with his own research work.

At the end of the first beer Paul said to me "Are you alright Nick? It doesn't seem like you're really talking to me. I know that's not like you. Normally you would have been keen to talk about travel, about getting back to Latin America, about getting up to good things. You've lost the spark, haven't you?"

I opened up to him about the trouble I had had since the separation, being left without anything, going through the bankruptcy first, then the divorce, seeing my children when I had enough petrol money to drive over to see them. I was full of woe. A proper sob story. He gently said to me *"Get over yourself."*

And he was right. I was getting in the way of myself and of who I am, and of who I am capable of being when I choose to be my best me.

I had lost sight of all the good stuff that I was doing, the great things that were present in my life but which, in that moment, were escaping my attention. He was completely right. I was angry at the world, frustrated at the pace of my life, annoyed at others who seemed to be living a golden life. I was whining about what I had lost, bitching about life being unfair. He turned me around and kindly pointed out that I had two great children, that I was renting a beautiful cottage in idyllic country-side, that I was working in a role I loved alongside people with a real 'can do' attitude of business start-ups during the day and working positively in the money advice sector in the evenings. He reminded me that I was in good health, had a great collection of books and music and that I had already achieved a lot in previous years.

That conversation with a good friend, where he could talk directly to me and point out that I was drag-ging myself down to a place that did not benefit me in any way, this was real friendship in action. It was a total turning point for me.

Many amazing things had happened in my life at that point to make it an incredibly rich one. In my career I had achieved national recognition and acclaim. My books had been well received and had generated a large income. The majority of the business investments I had built up were profitable ones and these had provided us with a very comfortable lifestyle. I had worked with many people seeking to develop their own success. But now, after bankruptcy, divorce and a serious downshift in housing, I had somehow lost the plot myself and totally forgotten to talk positively with myself about the basis of personal self-management.

An appointment with yourself is a way to get some good thinking back into your life and to create the space for creating some lasting good. You will not become debt free or even make much progress towards debt reduction without being clear in your mind that this is what you want and understanding the powerful reasons 'why' you want to be debt free.

STOP WITH THE PITY PARTY!

I had let my debts get the better of me. I had resorted to 'stinking thinking' and was hurting myself and those around me.

For a couple of years this was plain to see for anyone who was foolish enough to talk with me. All they got for their support and gentle encouragement was an ear bashing about the unfairness of life. How low I sank while my focus was on a personal pity-party! But this is why I can say nowadays that you must take the time to see quite how much you already have in your life that is good and positive. Put your focus on whatever gives you real insight into who you are and what is precious and special and important for you.

You have people in your life who are quite capable

of telling you how off-track you have been, if you will just let them. Such negative influence does you no good and you can get rid of these influences completely or begin to limit the time you send in such company through being aware that your diary is your own. Don't let your debt anxiety and money worry overload get in the way of you maintaining and nurturing those relationships with your friends.

TAKE STOCK.

Take a moment right now to acknowledge what you have got. This can be something that you write down as a list or can be a process that you simply think through, picturing in your mind all the good that you already have around you. I believe the actual process of writing this down is more powerful than simply thinking it through, because you involve several more sense if you are having to think, to feel, to touch and to see what you write out.

Take a walk around your home and see what you have in your space. Pick up objects that have real significance to you. This could be a photo of a special occasion, a book that helped you, a film which deeply moved you, a toy from childhood, or perhaps a piece of furniture with real memories. Count your blessings and realize how much you have going for you. Be grateful for what you have right now and welcome the additional good that is coming to you. Just be you.

. . .

LEARNING POINTS.

> You are not defined by your debt.

> Your main point of focus must be yourself.

> Stop with the 'stinking thinking'.

> Count your blessings.

> Be grateful for what you have.

FIVE

This is NOT the end of the world.

NO ONE HAS DEMOLISHED your home. Your car hasn't been rammed by a truck. Your work place haven't sacked you because of your debt. Your friends and relatives will still talk to you this weekend. You are not begging in the street. You can wash and clean your clothes ready for the next day.

You do have debts that you owe to some other people. But that's all it is.

These people do not wish you any harm. They know that if you can work, earn and live your life successfully, then they will inevitably be paid back what they originally lent you.

THE SUN ALWAYS RISES!

It is easy to feel scared, to worry about that pile of bills by the kitchen cupboards and to wonder where on earth the money will come from to clear those amounts needed. But you are OK in yourself right now, and the bills in each envelope are separate from you. There is money owed, for sure. You and the money owed are not the same things. One very big realization for you to make or to reach in your thinking is that the world will still function, and life will continue to go on even though you have debts which seem right now to be unmanageable. Bad stuff happens every day and you do not assume you are responsible for it. Difficult situations present themselves all day long in your life and in the lives of your friends, but these do not stop you from going to work, getting on with your day, or attending your family and social commitments, do they? You still make the effort to do the things you have said you will do. So why - when debt gets to a level that scares you - do you imagine that the end of the world is close at hand?

In this chapter I really want to get your attention about the fact that you have dealt with tough things before. Grief, dismissal from work, broken bones, the finishing of a loving relationship or the recovery from a long period of sickness. How did you cope with these blows to your sense of normality and stability? You will have got on with your life each day until a broken and upset heart turned into good mental health and the recovery of your self-esteem. Possibly the loss of a close friend or a family member knocked you for six for many months, perhaps much longer. Yet with the passage of time and the wisdom of experience you moved through this difficult time and you healed, you became more of yourself. What was a traumatic shock and a real pain for you is something that softened and became part of your life rather than taking over your life.

You are an amazing person, capable of withstanding dreadful experiences, of moving through awful life events and coming out the other side renewed, stronger and also wiser. My proposition is that debt is actually easier to deal with because you can measure the extent of it and are able to give it definition and dimension. Once you can define something - like the extent of your debt and the people or organizations it is owed to - you can have control of it, both emotionally and in a practical sense.

If this is true, that you can control what you can define, then surely the recognition of your debt situation means that rather than this being the end of the world for you it is in fact your opportunity to start afresh and to create a life that you can begin to design as you want it.

MONEY MATTERS - CHRIS.

Chris lived in one of my houses as a tenant. He was a breakfast chef in a city hotel and was working there after returning from a year in Spain where he had done a similar job in a beautiful resort on the Southern coast. He had been nervous around me in recent weeks, but I was not sure of the reason. His rent was paid-up, yet there was clearly something on his mind.

One morning when I was opening up my office in the building he stopped by and asked if I fancied a coffee. Sensing that this was his conversation opener about whatever was on his mind, I said yes, and he came up to see me. After some awkward silences he got around to telling me that he had been having trouble sleeping, that some difficult incidents from his childhood and which he had tried to hide or avoid, had recently begun to cause him difficulties. I just listened to him until he admitted that the night before he had just gone off to the hotel to work his late night and early morning shift, but had today experienced an anxiety attack in the kitchen and been sent home to rest.

Now he was panicking in front of me about not being able to cover the rent due in two weeks' time. He had decided to tell me about the situation because he had heard that I had gone through some difficult times with money, debt and job loss. He was stuck with an overdraft at the bank that he would not be able to pay if he did not go back to work soon. His brother had lent him $1,000 at the time that he had returned from Spain to tide him over for the period until he had got his new job.

So, he was caught in his fears about rent, a bank debt and a family loan, knowing only that he was unfit to return to work in the short-term and that he better tell someone fast. To him the world had ended with his anxiety attack the previous evening. He needed a lifeline and to talk with me about the difficulties he was experiencing.

Eight months on and the situation for Chris is different. He is still a tenant for the time being, although this may change as he has been making some good and realistic plans that will involve some travel again. He sought professional help for counseling about the issues from his childhood and found someone in the local medical network that he can talk with about this. I helped him submit an application for rent support from the housing office of the local council and agreed to a reduction in his rent figure. To put the bank debt and the loan from family into a less stressful place I drafted some letters for him to make into his own and then send out, explaining to them about his current situation with regard to having lost his job and offering some small weekly payments for the interim. Both creditors have accepted these. I sit down with Chris once a month to check he is still making his payments and enjoy a coffee together.

He has been through a tough time and had to open up about some very private things. But he is on a road to steady recovery while knowing that his housing is protected, and he is being supported professionally. He has not taken on any more debt and is starting to feel good enough to consider looking for work, still within catering but working more regular part-time hours. He has paid cash for a refurbished bicycle and uses this to stay in better shape than before. He has spent wisely on some low-cost coach trips to visit friends who he had not seen for several years. He is happier and feeling safer. Partly this is about facing up to some old worries that had not been dealt with. The other aspect of his recovery is due to the use of practical steps to dealing with debt, of communicating his situation clearly to his creditors and through committing to not taking on more debt.

. . .

YOU ARE OK.

Whatever your past was like, it is the past. Like that great cheery song by The Proclaimers, *'It's Over and Done With'* and which features in the uplifting Edinburgh based film 'Sunshine on Leith'. The past is not here now. You are free to move on. This is your today and you can do what you choose with it. There is no value in worrying about tomorrow as it will bring you no benefit.

How do you want your life to be?

What do you want things to be like on a daily basis as you earn money in your own business or work a job that you enjoy, doing activities and providing services that you enjoy being paid for?

In a month of work what do you expect to earn or how do you anticipate being rewarded?

Can you think about the lifestyle that you want to lead and see the link between what you want and the actions you take to move you towards this?

Give consideration to your living environment and where you make your home. You chose the life you lead now with every decision - conscious and also the unconscious ones - made up to this point. So if you start to make better decisions about what you want, where you want to be, about the quality of your friendships, relationships and work environment, then surely you will be creating and drawing to you the opportunities and people that matter to you.

STAY IN THIS DAY.

Today your debt is defined by what is added up from

the statements and demands for payment that are contained within those letters in your home. They have a specific value. They are simply numbers. You cannot pay them all today, so stop right now from living in the fear that you have to be dealing with each debt today. You do not serve yourself by living in a place of fear and inaction. The same is true for your creditors, as they are in no way served by your fear and uncertainty. As a lender of money I know from my own experience that I am always happier when a debtor is talking to me regularly and making small regular payments than when I hear nothing from them and am not receiving any form of regular or consistent payment.

Be focused on what the situation is today. If you have determined that you can pay nothing today, but that you can make an affordable payment towards one or more of your debts on Friday or Monday, this is fine. If you don't get paid for two weeks, and assuming you can cover your rent and food and transport to work, then don't spend these next two weeks sucking your thumb and feeling sorry for yourself. Get some letters or emails out to your creditors and keep them informed about when they can expect a payment. Make sure they know this is based upon you having some money on a particular date and tell them what payment you will be making to their account.

Until you can make the payment, don't live in fear of this being the end of the world. It is not. You simply have some debt. You either can deal with it today or you cannot.

· · ·

BE PRESENT.

Stay in this moment only and do what you can do now. Right now, you are ok. Be aware of your debt load but do not be defined by it. The time taken up by your debt each week or month is only small and should never be allowed to overwhelm you.

Let's say you have five separate debt amounts with five different creditors. Does it take five minutes once a month to do a bank transfer to each of the accounts? That's twenty-five minutes involved in looking at paper or email statements and responding with a payment. How about writing a letter or email to each of the five organizations each month? That's another twenty-five minutes. That's still less than an hour and you are actually doing something valuable about dealing with your debts.

Rather than seeing the world collapse around you, instead become more aware that you are making things happen and putting yourself back in control. One day at a time. This is how you climb out of debt. One day and one payment at a time.

LEARNING POINTS.

> Your friends and relatives will still talk to you.

> You and the money owed are not the same thing.

> Bad stuff has happened, and you survived OK.

> You are an amazing person.

> How do you want your life to be?

> Define something and you can control it.

> Do what you can in this moment.

SIX

Rebuilding - one brick at a time

GET THE RIGHT THINGS DONE.

When you start on a new project or a fresh initiative, you don't get to the finish point on the first day. You have to learn new ideas, acquire fresh skills and gain insights along the journey that you are making.

Getting out of debt is no different and so you need to apprentice yourself to the learning, to the different ways of doing things and dealing with money. In the chapters before this we have been laying the foundation for some new thinking, helping you to see that you got into debt from a mindset and a way of behaving that has not served you well.

Any new activity takes a while to bed in, to be accepted by your mind. If you've not been to the gym for a long time – or ever – it takes a huge commitment of energy, will power, and personal resolve to get yourself there and to put yourself through physical workouts that can seem daunting, difficult, and which will take consistent effort. You will put yourself through repeated routines before you sense the improvements of better physique and greater reserves of energy and stamina.

Getting out of debt and into a set of behaviors that support you into a new relationship around money does not happen overnight. You dig the foundation for a house long before you build the house above ground level, and you do this one brick at a time. This is how it is with getting you back in control of your money. Any effort to rebuild your thinking and your spending behavior is going to have you stretching and hurting in the early days of you changing from your previous money behavior. But the pain and effort of starting to do these things differently far outweighs the ache, the despair and the anguish of staying in the debting place and making no changes. Be clear on this now, just six months from now you can be in a completely different place mentally, emotionally and financially. Even three months from today you will be seeing big change by taking small daily and weekly action.

STAND BY YOUR DECISION.

You have done a great thing by reading this far in the book, and this section is about the practical steps to now bring about changes in your money thinking and your financial behavior. Others in your workplace, and perhaps in your extended family might not know about the personal struggles you have had with debt to this point. But in the privacy of your own home, when you are more alone with your own thoughts, you know full well the darkness, pain and suffering you have gone through with your debting actions. Allow yourself to really feel the difficulties, the awkwardness, the pain and the missed opportunities that have been caused by your debting. It was not until I admitted to myself the extent of my own action in causing the problem of the debting, that I could begin to relax as I became more honest with myself, simply accepting my role in the whole thing.

I had to yield to the weight of evidence around me. Such signs were evident all around me, in the form of creditor letters, doorstep visits, and calls from my landlord at the time about my own rent arrears. Once I acknowledged the truth of this, I could allow myself to let in the possibility of change and a new way of dealing with my debts.

In my later role as a debt advice worker I have attended several hundred house calls, seeing people at home to discuss their debts and to talk with them about the variety of potential solutions. I have witnessed the anger and denial of the problem expressed by the people I have been to see. It was almost as if there was a last-ditch attempt to deny the problem that they had admitted to when they had first called to book a home visit. They had backtracked, gone into a spin. Some people seemed to think that if they let go of their fears and admit to their worries, that they could be seen as weak.

Instead of such denial, the best way to deal with the situation of where you find yourself with your debt is to accept that by asking for help at this point you are actually showing your courage and standing up to the debt. It's as though you are now saying aloud,

"Enough is enough! There will be no more debt from this moment onwards."

From such a brave statement will come courage and the strength to deal with the problem. There is no going back from this point. You will win this battle and reclaim your financial peace of mind.

ACKNOWLEDGE the Reality of Your Debt.

Let go of your fear of the debt situation and allow something better to come along. You can only drive one car at a time, you can only enjoy one meal at a time, and you can only read one book at a time. You don't need to hang onto the idea of your debt weighing you down so much that you cannot enjoy any part of your day.

Your own route to becoming free of debt begins with you admitting to yourself that you have a problem with debt. The moment you do this you are allowing yourself to replace the fear and doubt of the debt difficulties and struggles to be replaced with something more helpful, more encouraging and to reach a solution that works for you.

Say it now :

"Enough is enough! There will be no more debt from this moment onwards."

SO, what practical steps can you make at home, at work, in your social life and in the way you think?

Practical Money Saving at Home.

A monthly and a weekly household budget is a good

place to begin these practical steps to taking control of your money. The idea here is that you establish an amount for what it costs you to run your house and all that goes with it.

Categories to include when you are attempting to work out your first rough calculations would be:

- Utilities -Gas, electric, water, council or local authority taxes.
- Food, clothing and entertainment.
- Leisure and holiday.
- Savings.
- Debt repayment.
- Let's take a look at these one by one.

UTILITIES - GAS, **electric, water, council or local authority taxes.**

YOU NEED to cover all these amounts but I'm willing to bet you can reduce the amount spent on several of these categories each week. Take the gas and electric utility accounts as easy ways to cut your costs down and release more money in your existing expenditure. If you use a timer setting on heating your home adjust the clock today to cut down several half hour blocks from your use of heating. Either you won't notice, or you can add a sweater or a an extra t-shirt under your clothing.

If your autumn heating is set to come on at 6pm would you notice if it came on at 6.30pm instead? If your home thermostat is set at 75F would you be able to function just as well on a more healthy 64F? I'm sure you would be able to function at the lower temperature, and would appreciate the lower heat bills when they come in.

If you look at the boiler settings can you turn them down to push out less power, completely separate from the main house temperature thermostat? For example, if your boiler heat output has ten settings and yours tends to sit at 7, try a week with it at 6. I'm willing to guess that neither you nor anyone else in the house will notice, but you will have a smaller bill from the gas company next month.

It's not just about what you spend on heating. How much heat are you losing from your home through poor insulation? A window or a door frame with a poor seal can lose you money every day in two ways. Firstly, because you are pushing heat through a gap in your building structure, but also because you mistakenly set the heating to a higher temperature than needed. For the sake of a few dollars you can insulate it with foam or padded tape, saving you more money.

Friends with a wood burning stove in their house were spending typically $60 - $80 a week on precut logs and collecting these from the farm store. By letting friends know they had a wood burner and would willingly take unwanted wood planks, logs, and waste wood furniture, they reduced their average monthly wood spend to half of what it was before. They cut their bills, heated their house adequately, and helped their friends by taking unwanted wood waste. Win - win. The amount they saved on fuel could be split between additional money thrown at debt repayments and placed into their saving fund.

FOOD, **clothing and entertainment.**

FOOD BUDGET.

A food budget is an easy and important place to start. Whether you live alone, as a couple or as a household with children you have a certain amount of money coming in and from this can determine a weekly figure. Draw this amount out from the bank or ATM as cash and place it in an envelope. Whether the amount is $60 or $50 dollars you work out the figure and then you stick to this amount. Also, make sure that you stick with the same day each week to take the cash out and place it in the food budget envelope.

The first week you trial the food budget make the time to go through every cupboard in your house and take out all the food that is packaged or tinned and stored there. What meals can you create from these items before you spend any more money? When we did this, we found two dozen tins of soup or beans, five sets of packaged cake mix, five packets of spaghetti, a dozen noodle meals, and enough other items of food to add the equivalent of one week of meals!

· · ·

CLOTHING.

One of the biggest debt builders in homes today are the crippling interest rates charged by the clothing catalogue stores, some of them funded more than a hundred years ago in the tradition of buy now and pay later mail-order. A $900 balance with a catalogue company can mean you paying $50 a month interest before you even add the minimum payment. Cleverly trapping you in debt while offering the promise that your mail-order wardrobe will make you look more beautiful or more handsome because of their well-designed clothes. Stop it now and don't buy into it. With interest rates often at 25% and more you must do all you can to get these down as fast as possible. Pay weekly rather than monthly to avoid the interest build up but get rid of them fast.

Review your existing wardrobe and have a clear out of the clothes you no longer like, never liked, or just no longer fit you anymore. Don't wait until you lose weight and they fit again. Get real and just let them go. Create space in your wardrobe for clothes that you are not paying interest on. You can take the unwanted and unneeded items to a thrift store or charity shop. You can wash and clean and take pictures of the best items and sell them slowly online. Take the cash you generate from such sales and spread it between debt and your emergency savings account.

Look at the quality and the volume of the clothing you have. Do you think you might do just as well with fewer clothes, but of a higher quality?

· · ·

SAVING **at your Work Place**

Coffee breaks, lunchtimes and social events after work. Any one of these can present difficulties or awkwardness that you simply don't need. A coffee-house cup can set you back a few pounds or dollars. Buy some instant coffee and keep a jar of this in your desk to make your own coffee for pennies. Take your own tea bags and soup sachets. Create a home-made lunch to your own taste every day or a few days each week.

By all means attend a work social event but watch your spending by leaving early or sticking to an amount of money for drinks or food, and only paying for your own. You can be present at an event and not incur more expenditure than you are prepared for. In becoming debt free you can communicate with workmates about your debt free journey and what it means to you and yours. Some of them will listen and learn from you. The opinions of those who don't support you are irrelevant. This is your life that you are seeking to improve. Enjoy your focus on your own situation.

CUTTING **costs on your Social Life.**

Invites to drinks parties, meals out, cinema and entertainment complexes. These are expensive events and places. Perhaps you have children at home and there is a steady round of birthday parties to attend or to host. For us this was a difficult time with the expectation of presents, gifts, party food or events. Sometimes it seemed like there was a different party to buy a present for every week.

The best memories seemed to come from the simpler parties and games held at home with friends invited over. Save where you can. Pick and choose the invites you accept. Becoming debt free is about achieving results for you and your family. It is not about pleasing anyone else.

A meal out with some friends can be a great evening and an opportunity to enjoy good company. If the event doesn't match your budget either decline outright and explain why or suggest a more affordable venue that you will enjoy. Accept such invites as you want to, but always considering it within your food budget for that month. Cinema events might introduce you to a great new movie, but their food stands can be outrageous in their charges. Take some of your own food or snacks and drinks and save from your budget.

My work colleague Tom takes a small bottle of whisky with him when out on a bar tour with friends. He will buy a soft drink and reinforce it with a dash of whisky. A $15 bottle of spirit translates to savings of at least $60 in the bars. I've done it myself and can vouch for the savings!

If you get a personal energy boost from sitting down to a good film in an independent cinema, or moving up a climbing wall, by walking through a forest in early morning, then you must protect these activities that lift you up and give you the energy and focus you need. If you love a bike ride through quiet streets early in the morning, or to play in a team game with good mates, then you absolutely must protect the money to replace tires on your bike, get new laces for your boots or new rope for your afternoon of climbing.

I hold the view that if you are restricting your budget so much that it bleeds you dry and leaves you as someone without scope for passion and expression, then you are on the wrong path to debt freedom. Within your budget make sure to set aside money for that which adds to you, fuels you, makes you the unique person you are. What value a reduced debt burden, but no happiness and a lack of spirit? Cut down on your costs and not on who you are.

CHANGES TO YOUR THINKING.

What value do you place on your own peace of mind? Practical changes here are less simple to determine and to define, but I would like to suggest that one very effective step you can take is to become more conscious in your thinking about money, debt and savings. You have an income from a job. Hopefully - because you want to have additional money to give yourself more options - you have created one or more incomes from a side hustle or part-time business that you run alongside your main work. Being reliant on just the one income is a potential problem waiting to happen in the event of a layoff, reduced hours, or the change to the structure of your workplace.

Being consciously aware of your money in and out, taking the time to track and monitor the flow of monies around you is crucial to success in achieving the necessary changes to reaching debt freedom. Success in reducing debt is like success in every sphere of your life - it requires you to work at it diligently and with focus. So, build time into your schedule to be aware of the money, to look at the bills and the statements associated with your Debt, your Earning, your Tax and your Savings activities.

You must not think that you will become debt free just by setting aside some of your income, or only by requesting the stopping of interest from your creditors, or even through the act of setting up some envelopes for separate household expenditures. No, you need to get yourself actively involved in each practical area of your money and how it functions in your day to day life.

Make time on a set day each week to look at your numbers in detail. This is your income for the past seven days and the predicted income for the next seven. Let me be as bold as to say that if you only have one job and you are paid monthly, that you should look at some other activities to create revenue for the other weeks of the month when you are not receiving money.

As a private landlord, as a writer and as a networker, I love the fact that I get a monthly income from my writing, but that we also get daily rental income. This happens because we have more than 31 tenants, enough literally for there to be someone paying their rent each day of the month! This was intentional. As I set up and developed a number of houses I was attracted to the idea of a good daily income.

With our networking business we also get a monthly bonus as well as a weekly payment for activity. When I had a job with a monthly salary, I got paid one day a month and felt like I was holding my breath for the other thirty days and dreading a large bill coming in. There's no need to be like that.

Can you look at your diary and set aside time to focus on your money flow?

How about some simple tracking notes or software to record the movement of your money?

Can you remove diary activities that don't make you feel good or support you earning?

Which day best suits you for a quick review of your Bank and Savings accounts?

You will create and develop new results by thinking in a different way about these important aspects of your life and getting yourself intimately involved in this journey to debt freedom.

LEARNING POINTS.

> A new way of behaving will take time to adopt.

> Be open to asking for help.

> Take on no more debt from this point.

> Find new ways to cut your costs and maintain your standard of living.

> Make sure that every money action counts for something.

> Take time to track and monitor your money flow.

SEVEN

A new debt free day is here

YESTERDAY AND BEFORE, you may well have spent a lot of time crying, worrying, being upset by the pressure of your debts. That's fine. I've got no problem with that, having been there myself with the sleepless nights and the anxiety about what might turn up in the morning post. But do you need to keep going there with it when it does you no good at all? You don't, do you? It took me a long while to learn this by trial and error. Now I see people able to deal with their debt faster because they can find a system that works for them.

KNOW YOUR DEBTS.

In truth, the simple act of knowing the extent of your debts - of being able to measure them and to know the individual amounts and the overall total - this allows you to know when you will be Debt Free. This is difficult to know if you stick your head in the sand and refuse to look at any of the detail. We are going to help you with this act of adding everything up, of recording and becoming clear about such numbers, but before you do this let's do something easy and enjoyable. Something that will help you and create some freedom in your thinking about the whole debt burden picture.

I really want to encourage you to start today with a new habit, and to help you understand that the establishment of a habit can be sorted within 30 days of repetition. Your brain is so used to going out and accepting your debting instructions that it will take a while for it to accept the decision you made to climb out of debt and stay out. You could try and pretend you have no debt, but your brain has been getting used to the idea. You might need a while to change that stinking thinking!

Here is your instruction for today.

"Today you do not take on any debt at all."

That's it. Today you incur no debt. You can of course spend money, but you take on no debt. It's important to understand the difference. Spending on what is needed, this is quite OK.

You do not have to borrow $3 to get a coffee. Make your own at home with what you have in the cupboards.

You do not put more into your basket at the grocery store than you can actually pay for in cash or on your debit card, without telling them you will settle at the weekend. No more running up an account. You will not use your credit card to buy anything.

You do not accept a cinema invite from a friend if you don't have the cash in your pocket for a ticket.

You will not let yourself use your credit card to buy

an item you see online or in a shop window or at the supermarket checkout counter if it means you taking on more debt.

Today you will add no debt. Not one penny. Not one cent of debt. Your Needs are Met.

I'm not asking you to pay any debts off today, just saying that you are not going to add to your debt today. Be clear on the difference. You have all the basics in place. You know the truth of what has been written earlier about you already having everything you need to survive. You have somewhere to sleep tonight, you have clothes to wear and you've already eaten. These are the basics that you need and which you already have. Sorted!

This is only about today. Tomorrow is not here yet, so let's not consider a day beyond this. Today is about making a massive, powerful, but incredibly simple shift in your money thinking and your debting behavior.

Your brain will likely be in turmoil at this final decision. Your excuses will be starting to fly thick and fast.

Beware of excuses.

Excuses and random thoughts like :

"But I need to pay my gym membership today."
"But I have to buy some new car tires."
"But the bank have told me to settle my credit card in full this month …"
"But I need to …"

These are all comments made in denial of the basic truth that you are in a mess and need to get yourself out of it. I've heard them all before and have tried a few of them myself. Recent excuses that I have heard voiced by my subconscious mind this month have included these.

"I want to borrow money to get myself a dealership financed new car."

I HAVE A PERFECTLY serviceable car that does a great job getting me around and which carries no debt. Why should I struggle to buy one that simply looks newer and costs up to ten times more?

"I want to borrow money from the department store to finance a new television."

I RARELY WATCH MORE than a couple of hours of TV in a week, so where this strange thought came from I really don't know! The last thing I want to do is lose several hours a day watching that.

"I need to buy a couple of sharp new suits, along with matching shoes."

I HAVE MANAGED to create a career and business interests for myself that don't require me to wear a suit. I already have a reasonable formal wardrobe for the rare occasions when it is useful or enjoyable to dress up.

.   .   .

IF ANY OF the thoughts that I have voiced to myself were actually significant I would take the cash out of a savings account and walk into the suit shop to try it on, or go to the car dealership and buy my next car with real money and no finance. But each time these thoughts surface I consider whether having the money in the bank gives me a better feeling than taking it out and exchanging it for something else to wear, drive or to watch. Each time the good feeling of keeping the cash in the savings account is the one that wins, and at that moment I know it was just my mind trying to play a game on me.

SO, stick with your promise to yourself.

"Today, for this one day, I will not debt."

MONEY MATTERS - **The Wisdom of Knute.**

PAY YOURSELF FIRST.

It took the calm wisdom of my friend and house-mate Knute, to help me get this idea into my head. I once shared a house with him for several months in Southern Mexico. He had gone through his own debting behavior as a younger man and then stopped himself, so he was comfortable telling me just how it was. He would not listen to my excuses. I had raged at the unfairness of the idea of a day in which I was not allowed to debt and I verbally kicked off with him at this.

He said to me :

"No, Nick. I never told you that you're not allowed to debt. I've simply suggested that you go a whole day without debting. Whether you do it is down to you and to your level of commitment to making a positive change in this situation that you want to let go of. What's it to be? Change or excuses?"

He had me there and I stopped with the excuses. All I was doing was wasting my breath and his time!

Knute had participated in a San Francisco debtors support program along the lines of Debtors Anonymous for several years and well before I ever met him. He was not ruffled by my frustration or moody resentment of his advice. He had worked through the principles of the debt recovery program attending regular meetings over four years to reach a point of no debt. His friendship meant a great deal to me and his advice is something I not only treasure, but am always happy to share - 'Pay Yourself First.'

In the years since regularly attending a debtor program he became a steady saver of a regular percentage of his income to the point that he had gathered together $180,000 of cash and shares or stocks. He had done this by making sure that each time he was paid he put a steady 10% aside first, effectively ensuring a payment to himself *before* he paid his normal household bills.

He knew that it worked to pay down debt and to rebuild financial confidence. He wasn't going to be upset by my tantrum. When I met him, he was successfully living in a lovely house in Mexico and using less than the interest on his investments to enjoy a good lifestyle in an amazing and vibrant community in Chiapas.

THAT'S a story of a friend making the transition from debt to freedom and a prosperous lifestyle. What about you? How can you make progress from the mess you are in now to the place where you want to be? Let's stick with this idea that you stop the debting and that you begin this with a day where you take on no more debt.

IT REALLY IS as simple as this. Your debts will only ever grow for two reasons.

1. You are being charged interest on what you already owe.

2. You are continuing with your debting behavior.

The first one is a separate step; one that can be dealt with later as we move through these ideas and practical steps to get you to where your debt is reducing and then goes completely.

Let's keep you focused now and for the rest of today on the second approach to debt reduction, that you *stop taking on financial commitments* that you are not actually paying for. Today you will take on no debt.

. . .

WHAT MIGHT **this Look Like in Reality?**

You have fuel in your car, so you don't need to buy more. You have food in your kitchen cupboards, so you eat from what you have. You have books on your shelves, paper in your printer, credit on your phone, clothes in your wardrobe, electric supply to your house and water supply to your property. So why would you need to add to your debt?

How about this scenario? A friend might call you up today and ask to borrow some money from you. This happened to me this morning while I am at home writing! A tenant texted me to ask to borrow $40 until their payday next week. If you have enough spare cash set aside for such a request and are happy with their repayment timetable, then of course you might lend the money. With my tenant, I was happy to make the short-term loan and did a bank transfer to her. I did this because I know her money profile and when she gets paid. I've lent to her before and was repaid within the agreed time.

It can be common that we might lend money to a friend or family member when we are actually not that financially strong ourselves. The reasons we do this can be complicated but are normally associated with the potential embarrassment we might feel at saying 'No' to them. We can occasionally make the mistake of lending when we shouldn't. But if you did not have the money to lend or you don't actually want to lend to them, then don't. A helpful response to use at this time might be to say something like *"I would like to help, but I have my available cash allocated to something else at the moment."* This can be a comfortable get-out phrase!

You might have a social gathering to attend. You can attend and only spend what you have or you can decline on the grounds that you know you might need to spend money on a credit card or borrow from a friend simply to be there. Not worth it so don't fall for that one. It's completely OK to say "I would love to help, but I'm already committed that night. Thanks anyway," and to keep hold of your money and your calendar.

A bill might turn up in the post this morning, but having a bill arrive and needing to pay it are not the same thing. Sure, you will pay it, but not today. Today is about ensuring you take on no debt. If you were to pay it today from existing funds in your bank account, then of course you can pay it, but if you were going to need to borrow to pay the bill then you do nothing with it today.

YOU DON'T NEED TO. You have committed to Climbing Out of Debt, to becoming debt free over a manageable timetable, so stick with your commitment to yourself. Just for today.

"Today, for this one day, I will not debt."

LEARNING POINTS.

> Have a day of no new debt.

> Pay yourself first by allocating money to savings.

> Stick with your commitment to yourself.

> Having a bill arrive and having to pay it are not the same thing.

> It's OK to say 'No' and keep hold of your money.

EIGHT

Where does it all go?

TRACK EVERY PENNY.

Being clear about your money is how you will become free of debt. Clarity over your finances, one day at a time, is where you start with this process and stop your debting behavior.

Today I want you to track every penny, cent or dime that passes through your hands. It won't necessarily be an easy exercise, but it will be a simple one. The reason that you need to do this is so that you know beyond any doubt where your money is and what the numbers look like. It's very common for a person in debt to not know the detail of the money that is passing through their hands at all. Not a clue. I refer to it as Debt Blindness, with the vision for any detail completely missing.

Try this for yourself. I'm going to assume that you know the cost of your rent or your mortgage payment each month – and if you don't then we have a real problem!

But how about the amount you spend at coffee shops

in a month? What about the cost of groceries on a Tuesday evening shop after work three weeks ago? How much did you spend last month on TV and Internet channels and magazine subscriptions? What did it cost you on your latest mobile phone bill? Do you really know? How much did you spend on car maintenance, servicing and parts these past twelve months? Scary questions? Am I getting too deep with the request for information?

DO I HAVE TO?

No. Is it OK for you to lurch from one unexpected expense to another and with no real sense of where you will get the money from to cover these? How about fear, embarrassment, shame, nervousness, guilt and distress? Would letting go of these emotional states be something that you would accept willingly in exchange for adopting and learning a couple of really simple approaches to dealing with your money? I do hope so.

Just for today carry a small notepad or a folded sheet of paper with you and write down exactly what you spend money on. To the exact penny.

Today my own notes look like this so far :

Car fuel	$40.00
Cappuccino	$ 2.80
Grapes	$ 2.00
Pastries	$ 1.40
Toiletries	$ 4.97
Laundry	$10.00
Total	$61.17

It's only midafternoon and I would expect to add some entries later for a meal out. Maybe some stationery for the office, possibly stamps at the Post Office. The more you log the full detail of your expenditure the less unconscious your spending pattern becomes.

WHY KEEP A SPENDING RECORD?

We get money in and we let it out. We rarely monitor it, analyze it, look at it for patterns, think about the movement, or consider much about it. But by the end of a first full day of monitoring this, your notepad will show you where you are spending the money.

Here's the other reason for keeping this Spending Record. It closes the gap between you and your money precisely because you are asking for a receipt for everything, and because you write down the cost of that latte before you actually take the first sip from the cup. If you enjoy it, you will appreciate what it cost you. If you have to write down the cost and then consider that you could have spent the money on something else for greater satisfaction or sense of value then the process of recording the spending has helped you to think more acutely about how you are using your money. Double bonus!

You have to take out your pen and note the cost of the newspaper or magazine before you turn the pages. You must write down the cost of the tank of fuel before you turn the key in the ignition to drive off. In each transaction you are noting the cost. At the close of the day tally up the numbers and see where you chose to spend money.

What do you see on the paper outside of the actual numbers? You get to identify very clearly the choices that you are making over what you want to spend your money on. It's right there in front of you. How do you feel about what you see? Notice your reaction to some of the things that you have spent your cash on.

So, here's a potential list from your spending day:

Cash	Coffee
Card	Stationery shop
Card	Bag of Groceries
Card	Clothing Item
Cash	Postage Stamps
Cash	Birthday Card

Next Steps after your Daily Record.

Now you translate this into a whole week with a summary of the previous 7 days of notes that you have made. Are there any items on the summary that might cause you to feel awkward or anxious about your spending behavior? This exercise is only for you. No one else is looking over your shoulder at this stage. It's your Spending Record. So if you see stuff on the lists that you think you could actually do without or perhaps buy less of, again it's completely fine to use this as a good reason to shift the direction of some of your spending. You cannot change a situation from a position of ignorance of the truth. Equally you cannot expect to change your spending patterns until you know what they are.

The first month I ever did the Spending Record exercise the thing that really upset me was how much I was spending on a can of beer here, a couple of bars of chocolate there, some fast food here, etc. In the course of a given week I could now see that I was choosing to hand over my hard-earned money for things that were my attempt to drown out my unhappiness about my situation. I was using a sugar rush to mask my upset about the way my life was. A few tins of beer each night was my attempt to paint over my feelings of not living the life that I thought I should be enjoying. But $4 a night on beer meant that $1,460 would have no chance to reach my savings account that year! I realized that the same $1,460 could do much better things if directed elsewhere.

Instead of looking after myself, treating myself to the relaxation of cooking a healthy meal after work, I was buying a container of fast food and numbing myself to the pain of what was missing in the way I was living my life. It was glaringly obvious to me that I was out of control. I was neglecting to make time for the pleasure of preparing my own food, and then enjoying a home cooked meal. By maintaining the Spending Record over the course of a day, then a week and across a whole month it served as a wakeup call to me. For this reason I regard the Spending Record as a very powerful habit for you to practice in order to give you the insight into your use of money, and then to use what you learn from doing it as a motivator to get yourself into a good place about getting free of your debt.

So, do it now. Do it today.

. . .

TOOLS TO HELP.

As a young man in my first full-time job I used the pages of a Filofax which came with lots of handily designed sheets to track money in and out. Nowadays, all types of journals and day planners exist to support you in monitoring to tracking your spending. Many of these can be bought cheaply at supermarkets as well as stationery stores, and the journal will often have a pocket in the back for you to keep tickets and receipts. Online software and apps for your phone make the ability to see pictures of your spending very easy indeed. You can just as easily insert spending items into your phone app and build up the spending pattern during the day, seeing it on a large screen when you get back to your laptop or PC. If you are visually motivated these tools will be a real help. If you are tactile in your approach, then pen and paper will be what works for you. The key thing is to find a process that is easy for you because you enjoy it. If it's complicated, you won't be giving yourself any incentive.

A pocket notebook that is easy to fit in your coat, or an envelope can both fulfil the role of a place to store your receipts. There is no need for you to spend any real money to capture the record of where you spend and what you buy with your money. The key is to make sure every expenditure gets logged somehow. If you buy with a debit card at the shop counter or the service station you will naturally be given a receipt. With simple cash transactions at the hardware store or in the green grocer shop you will either have to ask for a receipt or finish the purchase, reach for your notebook and write down what you just bought and the cost of it.

IF YOU'RE READING this at lunchtime you can still start to log your spending until you go to bed tonight. Tomorrow you can do a full day of recording the way that money is going through your hands.

SIMPLE RULES.

1. Record each expenditure. Don't miss one.
2. Write down the detail as soon as you can after spending the money.
3. Log the exact amount, to the actual penny.

IT'S REALLY simple to do this. From now on, you'll not put $50 in your pocket at the start of the day and then wonder at night why you have just $7.37 left over in change. You will know where the money went and what you spent it on. Your left-over cash and receipts will show you where the other $42.63 went during the day!

Maintaining the daily record and learning from the pattern of your spending in this way, puts you back in control, not just of your money but of your life. From knowing the numbers behind your spending, you then become conscious of your choices over what you buy. Only once you are fully aware of this can you start to make better informed decisions about saving, investing and further spending.

. . .

THE WEEKLY RECORD.

This is just a summary of all the information that you give yourself from the previous seven days. Keep it simple and make sure the numbers are accurate. So, run a week at the start of a month in the 1st day and include the 7th day. Start the next week on the 8th and include the 14th. Take you individual single day records and add them up to calculate the week.

If there are two of you in this exercise, then you need to each keep a record of your own and share them at the end of the week. It will be fascinating to compare notes and observations that you make as this week ends. Let's not even get into the issue of you perhaps having different incomes. We might be brave enough to approach this in another chapter! For now, you each keep your own daily, weekly and monthly records. Your combined goal once you've done this is to take a good look at the money and where you are spending it.

MONITOR YOUR PAPERWORK.

Your notebook or journal might not contain the whole truth. Because you have a bank account and may be running regular monthly payments or standing payment arrangements from it, there will be payments from the account that also need to be noted and included within your records. It's easy to overlook the passive payments in the background such as these, so check your bank account for the weekly record and ensure you have accounted for these when getting the full picture on your numbers.

Assuming you have a full and accurate record of where the money goes, you can divide the expenditure by 100 to create a percentage view of where you have spent your hard-earned cash.

Match the percentages against the categories that you can see within your spending behavior. Categories might be as general as House, Car, Clothing, School Fees, Food, Social and Holidays.

These would then break down in to:

HOUSE

Rent / Mortgage, Insurance, Gas, Electric, Water, Repairs, Laundry, Appliances, Taxes.

Car

Road tax, Insurance, Fuel, Valeting, Tyres, Accessories, Maintenance.

CLOTHING

Replacing worn clothing, Seasonal clothes, Boots, Shoes, Repairs.

SCHOOL

Meals, Fees, School Travel, text Books, Educational Trips, Club Memberships.

. . .

FOOD

Home, Work, Travelling Food, Gym Supplements.

Social

Dinners Out, Birthdays, Drinks, Events, Club Memberships and Gym Fees.

HOLIDAYS

Savings account for holidays, Food, Travel costs including air tickets and car hire.

IF BY THIS point you have begun the process of collecting the information on your daily and weekly spending, you will have made real effort to do this. Rest assured that this is a big part of the battle that is getting in control of your money. Now that you know where you have been spending you can confidently go forward, looking at why you spend where you do, and deciding on how you might want to change current spending priorities for some that potentially support you better.

LEARNING POINTS.

> Help yourself by tracking your spending.

> Your notebook will show you where the money is going.

> Find a process that's enjoyable because it is easy.

> The key is to make sure every spend gets logged.

> Check other monthly statements to include everything.

NINE

Getting organized

PULLING IT TOGETHER.

Spread across your home is the truth of your debt situation. I don't mean the psychological reasons for your debt. I just mean the actual specific detail about the amounts of debt and who you owe it to.

You already know from the work you have done on identifying your spending habits and from looking closely at where your money goes, that you can be in control of your spending one day at a time.

Today is about you pulling together all the information about what you owe.

This will be on official statements from energy companies, or on letters from collection agencies representing the people or organizations you have been ignoring. It might be on a sticky note on your fridge door, on a letter taped to the wall by your desk. Maybe you have a carrier bag of unopened mail stuffed behind the sofa, another bag pushed under your bed, and several more out of sight and in the back of a cupboard in the kitchen. We are going to look at exactly what you have been hiding for such a long time. Today you are going to find them all and bring them out into the light.

TAKE A DEEP BREATH!

You might well be trembling at the prospect of handling the bags, the envelopes and the folders that hold all these various debts. This is quite natural. After all, when we face any fear it makes us feel awkward, uncomfortable, nervous or downright scared. Millions of people feel the exact same way about the idea of confronting the physical evidence of debt. So go ahead, feel the worry, the terror, the sweats and anxiety about the process of touching - and getting physically in touch with all the evidence of your debting behavior. Today you are going to be very uncomfortable at various stages as you do this because you are getting in touch with something really big, your own debt situation.

Make a face. Scream and shout. Jump up and down on the spot. Run around the room, beat a cushion perhaps. OK. Have you got the adrenaline out of your system enough that we can carry on with this? Hope so.

Let's move on and do some practical things to change your thinking about a major part of your debting mentality. It's about dealing with that feeling, that inaccurate thought which you have allowed to rule you for so long. This work here is about you knowing the detail after so long spent out of control.

So, you've had your tantrum for the day? Great. Now we can get on with the program.

. . .

GO SHOPPING.

Yes! Get your shoes on, grab your coat and purse or wallet and leave the house.

Go to the nearest stationery store, or office supplies shop and start to browse the shelves that hold files and binders. You want to buy two of the larger ring binder files, the ones that you can place your debt paperwork in once you have used a hole punch for each letter or document that you choose to keep. You do have a hole punch at home, right?

The two large files that you are going to get and take home with you are very special. One will hold all the debt paperwork that you are going to keep. The second folder is for you to store all the bills that you pay off in full. For this task you need to choose for yourself two folders that are attractive to you because they are going to become very special items to you.

Another reason you want them to appeal to you visually is because you are going to have them *on display* in your home, whether this is on a shelf, on a cupboard top or placed neatly alongside your favorite books, music or household items.

A large ring binder can hold hundreds of sheets of paper so choose from the thicker binders. Make sure you have the two binders and a simple mechanical hole punch and then head home.

MAKE YOURSELF A DRINK.

Set up some good music and get all your debt paper-work out on the table. See this as a process that you need to work through in one go and realize that you may as well enjoy what you can of it. If you want help with this, then by all means get in touch with a friend who will help you sift, sort, shred, file and put in order the pieces of paper that you are going to keep.

Over the next few hours that you do this you might want to cry, shout, swear and curse, or laugh out loud. That's fine and is simply part of dealing with so many of the emotions stored up around your debt. You've got a coffee and the music is on. Open the first bag or box of debt paperwork. Pick up the first envelope and open it.

By the way, there will be a big opportunity for recy-cling envelopes and paper after this work is done so start to pile up the opened envelopes. Remember that friend with an open fire?

One pile for used envelopes and one pile for debt letters and statements.

OPEN EVERYTHING!

Do this until you have emptied the first bag or box completely. There may be others on the floor nearby and that is fine.

Right now, you have a batch of debt statements in front of you. This might be as many as 40 or 50 letters. Possibly more. They are unlikely to all be different. Let's say that they might be from ten companies and that you have four or five statements from each of those ten creditors.

Sort them into the different creditor sets. Let's say ABC Company have written to you ten times. Find the oldest letter and the most recent. Keep these two and discard the other eight letters.

Repeat this process with every batch or pile of letters. Keep the oldest and the most recent and throw out the ones in between. You don't need them.

From this example of five letters and ten creditors now you have just twenty sheets of debt statement and, of course, a massive pile of old envelopes and unneeded statements. Burn or shred the statements that you don't need to keep. Or put them in the trash to get them out of the house. The act of getting rid of so much of this debt "stuff" will clear a lot of the stuck energy in your home and you will soon notice the change.

So, you've removed the contents of one bag and gotten rid of it. You've sorted out and kept the oldest and the most recent statement or letter from each of these 10 sample creditors. Well done!

Remember your Alphabet?

Now get the hole punch and put the 10 sets of creditor correspondence into one of the binders. Do this so that you can find them again easily and quickly when you want to or need to.

So, if you have debts with:

PETE'S GARAGE
State Water Company
Town Energy Supplier
Debbie Jewelry Store

Adam Co DIY Merchant

AND SO ON. The paperwork is filed so the start of the alphabet is at the top.

You will have them filed now in alphabetical order like this:

ADAM CO DIY MERCHANT at the front, then behind it will be Debbie Jewelry Store, then Pete's Garage, State Water Company, and Town Energy Supplier. I'm sure you can see already where we are going with this.

The first four sheets or statements in your ring binder would look like this :

1	Adam Co DIY Merchant – most recent
2	Adam Co DIY Merchant – oldest
3	Debbie Jewellery Store – most recent
4	Debbie Jewellery Store – oldest

Where do I Find It?

With the storage of any paperwork it's not so much a question of "Where do I put it", but instead it's about "Where and How do I FIND it again?"

Keeping your paperwork in one folder and in alphabetical order is going to be so much easier than rooting through countless bags and boxes.

The binders need to be given a clear name. You get to choose, but the first one might be called CREDITORS or perhaps MONEY OWED.

The second file can be called BILLS PAID and will very quickly become your favorite of the two!

Both are very important and between them will come to be special to you for the way that they simplify your life and relieve you of some of the stress and exhaustion around the whole debt topic.

Now you have your two large binders, one for MONEY OWED and the other for BILLS PAID. It might take you another few hours, or a whole week of time gathered here and there when you can, to get the oldest and the most recent correspondence from each of your creditors and to get these into your MONEY OWED binder.

In the process of this you will continue to go through a lot of emotional ups and downs. You might experience lots of negative feelings towards yourself. Thoughts may surface like these :

"I CAN'T COPE with this. There's simply too much paperwork for me to handle."

"My house is such a mess and it's all my fault. I'll never be this organized."

"I can't believe I've allowed everything to get so chaotic."

"I hate myself for being so disorganized."

"I'm useless at this sort of thing. I'll never be able to get out of debt."

"This is just too much for me to deal with on my own."

.   .   .

IT'S NOT YOUR FAULT. This is a temporary situation. You will get more organized and in greater control. You can be tidier and still love yourself in the process! You can get good at being more in control. You can also get help with the process of dealing with your debts and becoming debt free over time.

Being brave enough to deal with the hidden paperwork, the unopened post and the real situation of your debts is something that you can move through and well beyond. You are able to put this part of your life in order and as you do so a great many other aspects of your life will see improvement.

DISCOVERING TREASURE.

In this very specific task of going around your home to find any pieces of debt related paperwork it is a certainty that other things which have gone missing will start to surface. Part of this is because when we avoid something that we are feeling awkward and want to hide it, we also push away other good things in the process.

As you move from room to room looking for debt correspondence and historic bills do not be surprised to find an old diary from a happier time, or some photographs that you thought were lost years ago. Among the post that you have not wanted to open and which you have stashed away, it is also very likely that you will unearth old love letters, find notes or pictures from your kids, discover old school reports, a journal, a scrapbook filled with positive memories, and a whole raft of bits and pieces from your previously well-managed and fully functioning life that you thought was gone.

This can include missing phone numbers or addresses of friends you have lost contact with. Often, when our debt worries overwhelm us, the first area of our life to suffer is our friendships, as we withdraw from our friends. It starts as a subtle thing, like not meeting up or canceling attending an event for fear of not being able to afford to pay our part of the meal or for the cinema tickets. After a few of these 'dropping-out of an event' situations, we can actually find ourselves stepping back from the important friendships that such events are simply a part of. We might pick up a voice message on our phone, but don't return the call out of worry that we might need to talk about the trouble we are having, yet fear doing so.

Don't kid yourself anymore. You need your friends. They want you, so let them in again. When you find a postcard or a note from a friend as you do your search for creditor letters, realize that maybe now is the time to be back in touch. They never know the extent to which you have been scared and they will be pleased to hear from you.

I mentioned earlier that you might come across an old diary or journal from better times. Often as our debt becomes a point of trouble and distress for us, we stop keeping a journal. After all, why would you want to make a note of how bad you feel in such a place of over-whelm? Have a rethink on this.

Today you might have purchased those two new binders, or you have managed an hour of opening and filing old post. You might perhaps have dealt with a whole shelf of stuff that needed opening, filing, or throwing away. Each one of these actions is an achievement for you and making a note of this - whether just for today or for a series of such activities - all of this is worth recording. It shows you are making a change, that you are taking a forward step, dealing with your debt one day at a time and putting yourself back in control of your larger life. One reason that I think of this as really important, is that there will come a time when someone asks you for help in climbing out of debt. From your own notes you can help them to see some of the steps you took to become free of your debt.

Remember that your debt is just one part of your life and that your debt is a temporary situation. So, keep a diary again as you go on this journey. It will inform you of the good steps you are making, allow you to see your progress and it might be a good source of encouragement later.

WHAT NEXT?

Your home should now be a less scary place because of the work you have just done. You have effectively given it a spring clean as you found and dealt with all the paperwork that relates to your debts and have kept the oldest and the most recent correspondence from your creditors. You must feel so different from the time before you started the process. The reason for this will be the confidence that has come from being back in control of your debt and no longer afraid of it.

. . .

ADDING IT ALL UP.

You have been really very busy recently! You've monitored your daily spending to the extent that you by now have a full month of your Spending Record. You have tidied up your home while rummaging around and looking for receipts, unpaid bills and all forms of creditor correspondence. These could be bank statements, garage bills, and invoices from the decorator or the carpet shop. No matter what they are, you know exactly *where* they are. They are now in your binder marked MONEY OWED!

Your life is completely unique to you and your debts will reflect this. If I see the MONEY OWED summary of 6 different households that I work with, then I expect to be looking at 6 very different sets of numbers in front of me. Each set of paperwork tells a unique story.

Here is a snapshot of a sample list of money owed. Yours will not be the same as this, but you will get the themes and will instantly recognize the importance of seeing everything down in writing.

Who You Owe	How Much	What for
Garage	$300	on car service
Rent	$600	arrears to landlord
Electric Company	$260	on usage in last quarter
Gas Company	$410	on usage in last quarter
Water Company	$110	for last 2 months usage
Decorator	$360	on painting of apartment
Butcher	$70	on outstanding bill
Brother	$800	Loan (No interest)
Parents	$2,600	Loan (5% interest)
Car Loan	$4,720	Remaining Balance (12% interest)
Furniture Store	$1,230	Outstanding account
School Fees	$2,310	remaining from last term
Bank	$1,000	Overdraft facility
Credit Card 1	$490	
Credit Card 2	$1,620	
Total Money Owed	$16,880	

So, from this paperwork exercise – and if these numbers were yours – you would know what you owe.

In this example, and that's all it is, you have the figure of $16,880 that is owed. Congratulations on getting to this point. Now you know the level of the debt you are dealing with. From here on you are in a great position to make progress on paying it down and climbing out of debt.

LEARNING POINTS.

> Pull together all your money paperwork.

> Shop for attractive binders to store your numbers.

> Be brave

> Enjoy bringing together all the documents.

> Create a filing system that will serve you well.

> You can be tidy and still love yourself!

> Celebrate the discoveries that will come with getting organised.

> Your debt paperwork is as unique as your life.

TEN

Back in control

IDENTIFYING TOTAL MONEY OWED.

You have invested the time to go through all your paperwork and to sort it into what is worth keeping, and what should be thrown away. From this you calculated your total debt. In the example we reached a figure of $16,880. You are finally in a position to define the extent of your debt load from your own unique set of creditor paperwork.

You also know that , based on your income each month, the maximum amount available for you to repay to your various creditors is $200. This allows you to stay safely within the numbers that your Spending Record has shown you to be sensible allocating to your category needs for Accommodation, Food, Heating, Insurance, Transport, Clothing, Leisure and Health.

Knowing this you can now look at the list of $16,880 as your Total Money Owed. You divide the Total Debt by 100 to give you the ability to identify what each creditor in front of you equals as a percentage of the total $16,880.

The resulting formula looks like this :

Total Money Owed = 100%

Play with the Percentages!

So, here is that list of creditors again, this time with a column that shows you what their separate percentage figures are of the Total Money Owed.

Who You Owe	How Much	What for
Garage	$300	on car service
Rent	$600	arrears to landlord
Electric Company	$260	on usage in last quarter
Gas Company	$410	on usage in last quarter
Water Company	$110	for last 2 months usage
Decorator	$360	on painting of apartment
Butcher	$70	on outstanding bill
Brother	$800	Loan (No interest)
Parents	$2,600	Loan (5% interest)
Car Loan	$4,720	Remaining Balance (12% interest)
Furniture Store	$1,230	Outstanding account
School Fees	$2,310	remaining from last term
Bank	$1,000	Overdraft facility
Credit Card 1	$490	
Credit Card 2	$1,620	
Total Money Owed	$16,880	

In the case of the $16,880 you divide this by 100 to give you the figure of $168.80. So, you know that every 1% of your total debt is $168.80. If you have identified that you can throw $200 a month at your debts, then you know that your debt would be reduced by more than 1% a month. Another way to look at this is that you can say for sure that if you put $200 a month against your total monies owed, then you would have paid it all off in just over 84 payments. This figure of 84 comes from dividing $16,880 by $200 and getting 84.4

WHEN WILL I be Debt Free?

Simply divide 84 (payments) by 12 (months in a year)

to get a figure of 7. It would take you 7 years to clear the $16,880 if you were to stick with repaying just $200 a month until all the debt had been settled.

"All your creditors deserve to be repaid in full."

Depressed again? Yes, I can relate to that. You know just what response you would get if you said to your brother or to the butcher that you will take 7 years to repay them. Not very positive, is it? All your creditors deserve to be repaid in full. So, let's look at the numbers again and identify another way to look at the same amounts. I think you will find this to be helpful and that it will give you considerable relief after how you felt about discovering the Total Money Owed figure. I don't want you to be overwhelmed, but instead to see that there is a way forward which you can enjoy and also look forward to.

By being clear about your numbers you are removing all uncertainty about the situation. This is the opposite to how we feel when we take the very different approach of ignoring our debt paperwork and living in fear. You can take great confidence from letting yourself know your numbers.

UNDERSTAND THE PATTERNS.

Here are your figures again. Now we are going to look at them from a fresh perspective. You will see a new column now, indicating which people or organizations are already receiving regular payments and those which are not:

Who You Owe	How Much	Monthly Bank Payment	%
Garage	$300	No	1.8
Rent	$600	Yes	3.6
Electric Company	$260	Yes	1.5
Gas Company	$410	Yes	2.4
Water Company	$110	Yes	0.7
Decorator	$360	No	2.1
Butcher	$70	No	0.4
Brother	$800	No	4.7
Parents	$2,600	No	15.4
Car Loan	$4,720	Yes	28.0
Furniture Store	$1,230	Yes	7.3
School Fees	$2,310	No	13.7
Bank	$1,000	No	5.9
Credit Card 1	$490	Yes	2.9
Credit Card 2	$1,620	Yes	9.6
Total Money Owed	$16,880		100

From your own regular earnings you are already successfully making Monthly Bank Payments that are going out regularly to half of these creditors as follows:

Who You Owe	How Much	Monthly Bank Payment	%
Rent	$600	Yes	3.6
Electric Company	$260	Yes	1.5
Gas Company	$410	Yes	2.4
Water Company	$110	Yes	0.7
Car Loan	$4,720	Yes	28.0
Furniture Store	$1,230	Yes	7.3
Credit Card 1	$490	Yes	2.9
Credit Card 2	$1,620	Yes	9.6
Total Money Owed	£11,750		69.7

Look at the difference now. Virtually 70% or way more than two thirds of your money owed is already being successfully dealt with by regular payment orders from your bank to the loan company for your car finance, to the utility companies and to the school, etc.

How do you feel as you start to look at the difference between Total Money Owed – which is what this exercise of gathering together all your paperwork has been about helping you to identify – and the monies that are not being settled or which are being paid only irregularly?

Can you see the benefit of clearer understanding that comes to yourself when you break them down into their separate parts?

. . .

"MONEY OWED and actual Unpaid or Static Debt are not the same things."

UNDERSTANDING STATIC DEBT.

The debt that is being ignored or is not being reduced by a regular payment is your Static debt. Let's imagine that the $600 to your landlord represents two weeks of your rent, where your rent is $1,200 a month. Is your landlord going to be ok with your settling this arrears figure over a few months? My guess is that although he or she would like it cleared, they will work with you to get it paid down over a few months. It's not that it represents a big risk to them as A), it is only a two week figure and B), you are making your regular monthly payments as normal.

As a landlord myself I accept that some tenants will occasionally have difficulties with their cashflow. The fact that they communicate this to me is helpful and I can always work with them to see a steady repayment of the rent arrears. Often it is not the amount that matters so much as the fact that the repayments are steady and reliable.

DEALING WITH THE STATIC DEBT.

Here are the numbers - taken out of the same total example of $16,880 - for the money you owe and where you have simply not been making or have not managed to make regular payments to your creditors. It is likely that these bills are causing you the greatest stress or are the biggest source of your worry. This is because they are generally to people or to small businesses that you see regularly or live close to or meet up with on a week by week basis. All of this can make things feel uncomfortable for you.

Who You Owe	How Much	Monthly Bank Payment	%
Garage	$300	No	1.8
Decorator	$360	No	2.1
Butcher	$70	No	0.4
Brother	$800	No	4.7
Parents	$2,600	No	15.4
School Fees	$2,310	No	13.7
Bank	$1,000	No	5.9
Total Money Owed	$5,130		30.3

Simply by looking at the amounts and the way you are dealing with them, we are now down to just 6 creditors and a figure of 30% or just under a third of your Total Money Owed figure!

YOUR PERSONAL RELATIONSHIPS AND DEBT.

If you take out or put to one side the $1,000 bank overdraft facility as something we can deal with in a slightly different way, you are left with 5 creditors who are local businesses, or family commitments. Of course, these are going to feel very personal compared to the big utility companies who you send money to each month. By removing that bank overdraft your percentage of Total Money Owed, and represented by these accounts, has dropped now to less than 25%.

Very often our own attention given to debts is as simple or as mis-directed as paying the person who shouts the loudest. So, the regular mailings and statements from organizations like credit card and loan companies or our utility suppliers seem to get our attention. Our payment behavior works in a similar way and we instinctively make our payments to the organizations before we think about repaying a friend or family member.

Why? Probably because it's easier to identify with a bill for something like gas or electricity because we need it to heat and light our home, so we know we had better pay it on time. That person al friend who lent us $300 or $500 can 'wait' because there is no particular urgency attached to the money and they don't write to us each month either! A lack of statements can be matched with a lack of payments. Does that seem awful?

A suggestion to paying down these 5 personal and close creditors with the $200 you have available each month would be as follows:

Who You Owe	How Much
Garage	$300
Decorator	$360
Butcher	$70
Brother	$800
Parents	$2,600
Total Money Owed	$4,130

The total to this group is $4,130 which, when you divide it by $200 (the amount you can repay each month), is the equivalent of 21 months. This way you would be settling in less than 2 years.

The psychology of debt is complicated enough before we take into account the additional burden of carrying debt owed to friends and family and to the small businesses in the community you live in and are a part of.

None of us want people to have a bad impression of us. The existence of debt will hurt and be a source of worry, embarrassment or guilt. So to help you deal with these concerns it is right to look at dealing with debts that have a personal or community attachment to them in a way that is different from the way you might approach a debt which is with larger or national organizations and companies.

This is assuming no increase in your core debting behavior, i.e. that you take on no more debt, and that you have a stable income from work or self-employment. If your income goes up - or you manage your costs and expenses down - you could repay faster. Alternatively, you could keep the new surplus to one side while building your savings account balance and stick with repayments over 21 months.

With the debt owed to personal or close contacts being $4,130 you know that 1% of this figure equals $41.30, so you can now see what percentage of this local debt is represented by each creditor.

Who You Owe	How Much	%
Garage	$300	7
Decorator	$360	9
Butcher	$70	2
Brother	$800	19
Parents	$2,600	63
Total Money Owed	$4,130	

Two ways forward here. You can either :

A) pay the creditor the Exact Percentage of the amount you have as surplus each month and see the associated debt decline steadily and slowly by that amount. You still have it all repaid within 21 months.

B) renegotiate based on your view of the risk involved in not managing the payments equally.

I would be tempted to go down the route of Option B here. This would see me paying off the butcher in full in the first month to clear that debt completely. With the remaining $130 I would pay the Garage all of the $130.

THIS WAY you can shop at the butcher free of guilt and worry, and you have made a big dent in the money you owed the Garage with more to come in month two.

Month Two liabilities would look like this:

Who You Owe	How Much
Garage	$170
Decorator	$360
Brother	$800
Parents	$2,600

You can now make a payment of $50 to each of the four remaining creditors, along with a note explaining that you have a set amount of surplus each month to reduce and eventually to clear these debts.

The garage debt would be paid off within just over three months. You then still have $200 surplus each month but now only three creditors.

The decorator would be settled and paid off in month eight, leaving monies owed to your Brother and to your Parents. Each of them would have received six regular payments of $50 per month since month three.

Your brother by this point is down to being owed $500 and your parents $2,300. But they have both seen the steady payments back to them and you have earned their respect for dealing with this effectively. From an example like this we don't know how you long it is since they lent you the money. I am willing to guess it is a year or more, so the relief for them that the money is coming back is very much a good thing. Their biggest pleasure though will be the knowledge that you cracked the whole repayment thing and the achievement this represents for you.

In month nine, because you have by now settled the smaller accounts, you could stick with $50 per month to your brother and increase the repayment to your parents up to $150 per month.

Your brother has been paid back by month 16. In that same month your repayments to your parents have reached $1,300 (6 x $50, and then 6 x $150). This is good going against the original loan of $2,600 and you have just $1,300 to settle in full. You are exactly halfway there. Now that you have cleared the other smaller creditors completely you can enjoy the knowledge that you will clear the final $1,300 in just 6.5 months by using all of the available $200 each month.

From this example, *and that is all it represents,* you can perhaps see why a bit of flexibility in the repayment to people you know and who are in your community can make more sense than a rigid, fixed, or set percentage amount, which I find works better – and is more frequently understood – by the larger or more corporate creditors.

In this example list I created I can imagine that the

garage who are owed $300 and the butcher who is owed $70 might be the ones who would be the least welcoming of a proposal to pay tiny amounts over a long period of time. It doesn't mean that they will not accept such an offer from you. I just think that as small business owners and possibly as people you know well in your community you might have the greatest trouble or the highest embarrassment in attempting a slow and steady proposal like that.

One of the other advantages to this approach is that you get to see whole accounts settled in full along your journey and you get the satisfaction of taking the statement or balancing numbers for that account and writing PAID IN FULL across that statement before filing it in Binder number Two, the one marked BILLS PAID. This will become such a special binder for you, tracking your forward progress.

With the percentage figure paid to each creditor every month and with no deviation or leeway from that set process, you of course get out of debt in the same period of time, but you settle every debt with a final payment one year or three years or six years from now with far less total wins or payments in full along the way.

This is where you have choice and freewill and where you get to decide the best route for you.

DEBT SWAPPING.

Sometimes this is a good solution to the example I shared earlier i.e. where the butcher and the garage are non-institutional creditors and you want to settle them quickly. You might consider it better to borrow the $370 to settle the $70 to the butcher and the $300 to the garage. The debt has not changed here, you have simply added it to someone or somebody who you already owe money to, perhaps the brother or the parents in the example we used. Or you might explain the situation to a good friend, about how you owe the money to the two small businesses and instead borrow the $370 from them on an agreed repayment program.

By debt swapping you can keep the debt the same but work with creditors who better understand the situation you are in, and who can give you some flexibility that was not possible with the original creditors.

WHEN WILL I BE FREE?

We all want to know when this awful, painful situation will be over. We want to be rid of the negative emotions that have followed us on our debt journey.

Simply divide the amount owed (in the example case we found $16,880) by the monthly amount that you can repay from your Monthly Budget. Then divide the new figure by 12.

So $16,880 divided by $200 is 84.4 months. Divide this by 12 and you get 7 years to be debt free.

How Long? *"Seven years! My creditors won't wait that long for their money."*

They will wait. Not only will they wait, but they will appreciate that you are doing all you can to deal with the situation. So many times they get no response to their calls or letters so to have contact from a debtor who has a realistic plan for becoming free of debt is a genuine relief to them.

You calculated that $200 is what you can repay, and this is the figure that they will rely on being shared among them all. So, stick with it and know for sure that in 84 months from now your situation will be behind you.

In countless examples I have seen that the original time calculated (from identifying the Total Debt and the Spending Budget) to repay the debt, ends up being much less than first worked out. People get a promotion at work or an annual pay increase, or an uplift in their hourly rate of pay. They receive some birthday money or Christmas money. They get to take a close look at the items in their house and which they no longer consider necessary or useful. They sell them online and raise considerable funds to split between a savings account and their debt repayment or Debt Freedom account.

Could you raise $2,400 in unwanted household items over several months and cut perhaps a year from your scheduled repayment timetable towards becoming debt free? What do you have in your house that is not serving you very well, or which you use only very rarely or not at all?

How about earning an extra $50 a week from a part-time job that again cuts a further 6 months from your debt repayment plans, enabling you to be free of debt months earlier than you originally envisioned?

Don't kick out at the fact that you have the debt and that it will take time to pay it down. Instead, look at this as a time to be creative, inventive and thoughtful about the many ways that you can get each month paid off sooner. Get the whole household involved by explaining how things can be different and better by considering what you might be able to let go of via online auction sites in exchange for money that can be split between a family or household savings account for definite benefits and reduction of debts.

Keep your focus on the reasons why you will feel so much better by clearing some of your debt each and every month. Acknowledge the importance of also gathering some savings at the same time to be used and enjoyed on things you will all enjoy.

This is your debt so you can get to choose quite how you deal with the terms of repayment.

You need to remain organized and in control of the numbers so that you can give yourself the relative freedom and the knowledge that you are getting yourself out of your debt situation, stepping away from your debting behavior for good. Becoming free of your debt one monthly payment at a time is the easiest way to achieve all of this.

LEARNING POINTS.

> Each creditor deserves to be repaid.

> Debt owed to those we know can be the slowest to settle.

> Local and family debt is going to feel very personal.

> The psychology of debt can feel complicated.

> Money Owed and Static Debt are not the same.

> It's OK for you to settle some debts faster than others.

> You can gain some flexibility with Debt Swapping.

> Look at this as a time to be creative, inventive and thoughtful about your money decisions.

ELEVEN

Communicating with confidence

YOU NEED TO MAKE REPAYMENTS, of course you do! Beyond this you must have regular contact with the people you owe money to. To my mind. good communication is the single most important behavior you need to master in all the lessons shared with you in this book. If a creditor knows that you are in steady contact with them, they have less worry or concern over whether they are going to be repaid. Whether it is with a text message or email to close friends and family where such an approach is OK, or by a letter or email to a larger and more formal creditor organization, you need to find the correct method to communicate and then stick with this regularly.

GOOD COMMUNICATION MATTERS.

It goes further than simply being massively important. Let's say you make a call to a store creditor who has written to you about an $800 outstanding debt on some furniture. You bought the furniture last year and should have paid this final amount off by now. They want you to settle in full next week. In the call you make clear that you are sticking to a budget and that you can only pay $30 towards the debt this week and you will make the payment on Friday and that you will then make this the regular weekly figure to be transferred every week on a Friday.

You have the call with a lady called Marilyn Fonseca in their accounts department on a Tuesday afternoon. She does not want to accept the smaller payment, but you go back and forth in conversation until she understands that this is all you can pay from your budget. She accepts this figure and the weekly payment. She does not want to agree to a long term arrangement that you can pay $30 a week until the debt is cleared (this would take some twenty seven weeks), but she does say that the business will accept your offer of $30 a week for two months and then review this. What is happening here? They are getting a sense of a regular commitment to have the debt cleared and you have won a result that fits to your household budget.

MAINTAINING ACCURATE RECORDS.

Now you need to create a record of this information from the call. In your Money Journal or with the letter from the furniture store, you write a note directly on to the statement they sent you.

It might simply be :

Monday. Feb 12. Telephone conversation with Marilyn

Fonseca. Accounts Department. 2.30pm. She accepted $30 a week for next two months. To be reviewed mid-April.

Having done this, you file the statement in your folder and the record is there for you to see next time you want to refer to it. You don't need to remember the detail because it is written down and there for you to refer to at some future point when the discussion comes up again.

Now you write a quick letter to Marilyn Fonseca, thanking her for her time and for accepting your offer of $30 a week for the next two months. Date the letter, make sure you reference the date of your call and your storecard account number, and get the letter out in the post as soon as you can, Preferably the same day or the next. Print and file a copy of the letter and put it in the folder on top of the furniture company statement. Either on the statement or on your copy letter list the dates of the next eight Fridays and put $30 against each date. Each time you make a payment reward yourself with a nice red tick against the payment. You must control the record of your communication and the record of your payments made. Then jump into your diary and make a note to Review Furniture Store Debt eight weeks from now. Set a reminder alarm on your phone or laptop. Then forget about it until mid-April.

Whether you are talking with utility companies, the bank, your credit card provider, the local car dealership or the revenue service, make sure that you keep a record of the dates of the calls you have with them and the name of each person you speak with. In some organizations you will get just the first name as some companies have a policy of not requiring the staff to provide their family name. This is understandable and where there might be several people with the same first name you will often be given an initial or a reference to a unit or team from within the call center.

The letter and the record of calls made is good with external businesses, large organizations or the power company. This process is obviously going to work in a slightly different way if Uncle George lent you $1,000 for a car repair bill or if best friend Stephanie loaned you $400. Family and friends need a slightly different approach to keep them close and informed through good communication.

You still need to keep a record of any call or text or conversation you have. The personal call is often more important than the digital message, but you must also record the payments that you make.

PUTTING IT IN WRITING.

Let's look at the $400 borrowed from your friend. You were short on paying some bills two months ago and knew you would struggle. Perhaps your friend heard how worried you were and offered to help. She provided the $400 for two months and you agreed between the two of you that you would pay back $200 on your first payday after borrowing and the remainder on the second pay day. Of course, this didn't go to plan and you only repaid $100 the first month and now owe $300. Steph wants her money back as soon as possible, but neither of you want to fall out over it. You value her friendship and want to record what you have said to each other about the $100 you missed and how you will now repay that plus the other $200. I am going to assume here that she knows why you only repaid $100 to start with.

You can drop her a quick email that perhaps says something like this:

DEAR STEPH,

Thanks for being understanding about the smaller repayment of $100 that I made to your account last week. I know I had expected to repay $200 but just was not able to.

My next wage payment from work is in three weeks time and I will give you $200 then.

This leaves $100 from the original amount of $400 you lent me.

I have some overtime coming up next weekend and will give you $50 from that extra work in about two weeks' time. For the remaining $50 I will keep in touch and let you know as soon as I have some accurate sense of when it is coming in.

Thanks again for your help and support.

USE YOUR OWN STYLE, your own words and energy, but at the same time ensure you have a record of what you have paid back, against how much your originally borrowed, and give them some sense of how you will settle what is owed. The staying in touch and being responsible for the communication is your job. They lent you the money to help you out of a tight spot, so the very least you can do is keep your friend updated about what the expected timings are for your repayment of the personal loan.

TAX AND THE REVENUE SERVICE.

There is a time when you need to prioritize some of your debts. (In England where I live and work, a person can be imprisoned for stubborn refusal to pay either their local Council Tax or the monies due for tax reasons to HMRC - the tax and revenue service. Yes, this is an extreme outcome, but it remains an option for the authorities). So, it makes sense when dealing with your creditors, that if these two categories of debt - tax and the revenue service - are in your list, you will make an effort to correctly deal with these as being very important. They are a part of the framework of your economy and they have a lot of power. A statement generated by - for example - the Revenue Service, needs to be taken as seriously as any other creditor, and then some more.

It is important that you stay on the right side of them and, just as with any larger creditor that you deal with, it is vital to connect with a person in the organization. The larger the size of the group you are dealing with, the more important it is that you find a human contact as it is otherwise easy to get lost or to feel somewhat out of control. Several self-employed clients we have worked with owed larger amounts to the Revenue service than they could settle quickly and so they agreed a weekly payment arrangement over several years, adjusting it up or down with each tax year assessment and making additional payments each time they could afford to.

The knowledge that they would be receiving regular weekly monies was enough in each situation to give the Revenue the comfort to accept these separate proposals from different traders. In this respect they as a creditor are the same as all your other creditors, something steady is far better for them and their cashflow than erratic or occasion payments would ever be.

COLLECTING A DEBT COSTS MONEY.

Consider this. It is an unpredictable and expensive process to issue a statement of debt to a person, and to then have to chase the debt with repeated letters, phone calls and potentially the use of collection agents. If you have a debt and make a commitment to regular and steady payment - be this monthly or weekly - then your creditor knows that they can collect the debt in without the cost of these additional resources being employed. So, writing well-structured letters, that detail your income & expenditure and clearly explain what you have as available disposable income for debt repayment, such letters are incredibly valuable for you. They work on your behalf to communicate to your creditor the intent you have to settle your debts, albeit slower than the originally agreed timetable. Get behind the letter process, giving confidence not just to you but also to your creditor.

With any tax monies due, first be clear that you do

in fact owe the amount that is being requested as payment by them. Have you checked their calculations? Have you been sure to claim all the relevant allowances and tax incentives that you qualify for? If you are unsure about how the tax authority has calculated the figure, then speak with a suitably qualified friend about the figures involved. This ought to be an accountant, a bookkeeper, or a business owner who understands the tax system.

THIS IS AN AGREED TRANSACTION.

As you negotiate with each of your larger creditor institutions keep in mind that you are equal to each other in the arrangement that you make between you. They want to see the return of the money that you borrowed, either as a loan or to the value of the products that you bought and which you have not completed paying for. You want to negotiate a repayment figure or amount that you can afford and which you can stick with each month. Your own professionalism in this process of arranging a repayment is essential. This is even more so where emotions might be running high for either of you. Stick to the topic of the money as the main point of focus. Avoid getting into any tantrums or arguments about the rate of repayment perhaps being slower than your creditors might want in an ideal world. By making the contract with them, by laying out the details of your total money owed, and by showing that you are repaying your debt in a proportionate way to your income, you can take the emotional issues out of the conversation and show that you are getting on with the process of clearing your debt.

STAND YOUR GROUND WITH CONFIDENCE.

Don't allow yourself to be bullied. Sure, you owe money. It is easy to think that the company that lent to you has the power over you, but don't fall for this. You can make an arrangement over your debts. You can make regular payments that match your budget. By doing this you are maintaining a debt reduction program that is affordable and manageable. Back yourself up with a completed Financial Statement that clearly illustrates income and expenditure as well as total liabilities.

You are engaging in the process. You are committed to seeing the total repayment of the debt within a manageable timeframe. This means within a schedule that is manageable by you. They might want payment faster of course, but this is about you and your resources and you being able to maintain a consistent repayment. You have shown up to be accountable and responsible for the repayment. With smaller creditors in your community, and with family members too, a lot of the discussion is likely to be face to face and over a coffee. With the banks and the finance houses and loan companies, things will be dealt with by telephone and the paperwork will move between them and yourself.

You are a completely equal partner in this negotiation and in the agreement that you are making with your creditors. So, own the process. Own your involvement and your responsibility for this.

ALLOWING FOR INTEREST.

Interest at a manageable rate is something that you can deal with. Where it is excessive and preventing you from repaying the original debt amount you have choice. In a situation of compound interest that is sabotaging any opportunity to repay the principal amount owed, you may be best positioned to have the interest stopped or frozen on the borrowing. You can request this, and always do so in writing.

Your lender will understand that it is better for them to see the steady repayment of the loan, rather than to have you personally hurt so much by your debt burden that you are unable to repay. For them as a lender it is crucial to at least recover their original money, so they can relend it to someone else. The interest earned is the reason they are in business, but they will always want to protect the initial capital.

A typical letter to request the ending of interest being applied to your borrowing can be something like this :

DEAR SIR,

My account number 7246-1235-3423-1738 Credit Card

I have received the latest statement from your organization dated as at February 18.

It shows a debt of $1,823.47 and this figure includes accu-

mulated interest of $47.94 that was applied to the account over the past month.

My personal situation is that I am on a low wage and working part time hours.

I have included a detailed account of my Income & Expenditure. From this you will see I have a total monthly income of $1,134 and that my expenditure each month is $962.

This gives me an amount of $172 each month and this is all that I have to use across all of my creditors.

With my existing debts owed and attached in a separate written list you will see that my debts equal $6,348.

From the $172 per month that I have available I offer to pay you $50 each month until the debt is cleared in full. However, as part of this intention to settle the debt owed, I formally request that you immediately cease charging interest and administration fees on the account.

I have made the offer of $50 per month based on the fact that this represents ca 29% of my disposable money and that my debt to your organization represents ca 29% of my total debts of $6,348.

This offer to repay based upon my total available income is being made to each of my creditors and the success of my repayment proposal is based upon each creator accepting my offer.

I will make my first payment of $50 to you at the end of this week and repeat the payment amount each month until the debt is cleared in full.

I trust to hear from you with your acceptance of this proposal.

Yours faithfully, etc.

.   .   .

SOME FRIENDS and purists within the debt free community hold occasionally to the view that you should pay back all the interest, but I disagree on the grounds that I believe every penny should go to the debt rather than the debt plus potential interest charged. The value of correspondence to your creditors in which you request the stopping of interest and additional charges being added to your original debt is of huge significance. Consider the massive extra load that the interest burden puts on to your repayment schedule. Fight hard to get the interest stopped. This does not mean you being aggressive, rather that you are persistent in putting forward your case of seeking to deal with the original capital amount that was lent to you.

If you have borrowed from a higher rate of interest money lender, or a "payday" lender, then it is best that you seek specialist money advice guidance from a state or local city organization like the Citizens Advice Bureau. They can help you in getting the debt listed or reported as unaffordable by yourself.

In the case of illegal money lending by some door step lenders or loan sharks you can have the supportive involvement of the Court system, having the money you borrowed logged as being at excessive rates and request that – if you seek to repay the initial amount borrowed – this is done via you paying through a Court or mediated channel rather than having to have any further dealings with the original lender.

Where you have borrowed through legitimate lenders with a valid credit broker license, you have the scope to request and negotiate the removal of interest from the original borrowing and to focus on repaying only the principal or original loan amount.

LEARNING POINTS.

> Protect yourself by keeping good records.

> Your creditors respect payment and good communication.

> You don't need to remember detail that is written down.

> Keep detailed notes of creditor communication and of payments made.

> Be persistent in getting interest stopped.

> Stay in regular contact with your creditors.

TWELVE

This is your debt, so own it!

THESE ARE YOUR NUMBERS!

The numbers on the income, expenditure and debt pages of your money journals and notebooks will show you exactly where you are. These numbers are yours. They indicate very clearly that this is your debt. You took it on, consciously and at times unconsciously, with each purchase, loan or request for financial flexibility when you thought you had to. The statements and the loan documents and the utility debts each have your name on them. You look at these documents and the numbers on them and the truth is plain to see. This is your accumulated debt. It belongs to you. As such you are the person to whom it has the greatest meaning.

When you talk with the family and friends who are owed money by you, show them your total debts, your budgets and your record of what you need to live on and what is left over to be used for payment to creditors. As people who know you well they will likely be the most supportive or understanding of your efforts to become free of debt, and they will listen as you explain your intended repayment timetable and the level at which you can make payments.

Yet for all their attention or effort, it is **you** who has the greatest emotional connection with the numbers. Remember that it doesn't so much matter what you repay each month to begin with. Instead the crucial issue is that you can sustain these payments week after week until the debt is repaid and you can strike that particular one off your creditor list forever. Maintain whatever weekly payment you can to family and friends and keep talking with them.

Where you are most likely to get resistance, stubborn attitudes and possibly an initial lack of cooperation is within the larger organizations, finance houses and retail stores that you have incurred debt with.

MONEY MATTERS - WALDO.

Waldo was a tenant of mine. After a split with his girlfriend he moved into my house, in which I had a couple of spare letting rooms. Over a few months his own story of debt and financial trouble came out in little conversations here and there as we moved around each other in the house. He spoke English only as a second language and was still learning new vocabulary from a pocket dictionary he carried around with him.

The exquisite white leather sofa and chairs, the smoked glass coffee table, and the brushed steel frame of his king size bed had come into the house with him when he moved in. It came out in chats over coffee that

he had borrowed the money for all of this to accommo-
date or to impress the woman he had subsequently
fallen out of love with shortly before becoming my
lodger. Grossly overpriced he had bought everything on
credit for $3,500. On a low paid job in the warehouse
team for a national supermarket, he was juggling his
wages to cover his car and living costs, while also finding
the rent money.

When he asked for help it was easy for me to call the
department store on his behalf and reduce the
payments. This way he extended his repayment term
from 12 months to 24 and halved his payments,
meaning that he could keep a small surplus each month
from then on.

But the effort involved in getting the better deal and
the extended payment schedule took some doing. He
had to submit an income & expenditure statement, and
supply copies of his pay slips to prove that he was no
longer receiving the regular overtime pay that he was
getting when he first bought all the furniture. After these
documents had been supplied to the credit department
in the store, they still rejected the request for a reduced
payment. Their argument was that he had said he could
afford the monthly payments at the time of purchase.

This was the point at which I called on his behalf,
speaking first to the credit control officer who was
blocking Waldo's request for an easier payment. We then
found a person on the same team who was better able to
grasp the issue that he could genuinely only afford what
he was offering, and so the new agreement was made.
His intention to deal with his debt was hampered by his

poor language ability, trying to negotiate on technical terms in a second language is not easy.

FIND **the Person who will Listen.**

When dealing with the larger organizations, call them regularly until you find the person who seems to be listening to you, who is considering your repayment proposal seriously. For any large creditor it is of course easier for them to agree a nice tidy package with you and to receive just one automated payment from you each month. That might well suit them and tick the current box within their credit control system, but it doesn't mean that it suits you and your budget, spending record or repayment plan. This is your debt so you need to step up to the line and deal with it, fight for its reduction under terms that you can accept because you know you can manage the repayment schedule or the numbers that you commit to.

If you owe $2,000 and know for sure that you can only repay $13 a week over 154 weeks based on your actual weekly wage right now, then you go right ahead and sell them on that model of repayment. They might reject the proposal so pay them anyway! Transfer $13 to their correct bank account and with the proper allocated reference number for yourself and do it this week. Do the same again next week and the week after.

Each week call the Credit Control team or the Customer Finance team and connect with someone who can see that you are good to your word, that you have been making the payments in line with your initial proposal and which was already well thought through when you first made the offer to them. (Log the details of when you call and who you speak with). Just because it is not what their computer or their pro-forma template tells them they should be receiving, this should not prevent you from making steady repayment until you have created your own evidence of your reliability through the act of making those payments.

OFFER **only What You Can Afford.**

I repaid an $1,100 Council Tax bill at $30 a week because it was easier and more manageable for me to do this weekly than worry about whether the $130 a month that they wanted in a single payment would clear the bank. They declined my offer - made to them by telephone - to pay $30 every week and said it as unacceptable to their credit control team. So, I paid $30 the next day anyway.

Seven days later I repeated the process. After six weeks of this I called them up and explained that I could not manage the risk of one large amount coming out of my bank account, in case of poor cash flow coming in that day. I asked them to confirm they had received my six payments and requested that I continue to make payments under the same schedule. Of course, they accepted it based on the steady pattern of payments they had already seen. This approach works because they see that you are delivering on your regular payment promise.

MONEY MATTERS - MARINELA.

Marinela is a tenant who wanted some help in drafting her response to the Collections Team of her phone company, and to the local authority over the issue of a Council Tax bill that had been incorrectly calculated. The fact is that these large organizations can be very bureaucratic, and you need to work at communicating with them in the first instance, and then at making sure they understand and accept your proposal.

In the previous six months her income had changed downwards when she moved from a job in a busy commercial restaurant. In that job she was receiving a decent wage, frequent overtime, and often getting good tips from the pot that was shared with other staff. One downside of the role was the high cost of getting a taxi home when she worked late. Keen to cut her costs she moved from a more expensive apartment to a rented room in one of my houses, and took a job working just daytime hours in the restaurant of our local court building. By doing this she lost the opportunity to earn overtime and receive tips, but she has more energy and has got her social life back by cutting out the long hours. She now also cut out the costly taxi rides home late at night.

Marinela's offer to the phone company was rejected the first time. They wanted her to clear a bill of $475 in three months which she absolutely could not do on her reduced earnings. So, she made weekly payments at a rate that was realistic and sustainable. She cleared the debt in 42 weeks instead of the 12 that the phone provider had requested. She went against paying what the phone company wanted, and instead she made her own calculated and affordable payment weekly. This is what allowed her - after two months of regular weekly payments - to secure an authorized extension to the repayment program.

With the overcharged local tax she had to spend a lot of time, both in correspondence and then in a face to face meeting at their offices, to evidence to them that the bill should have been significantly less. By adopting a professional and non-confrontational approach with each creditor, she was able to clear both debts in a time frame that worked for her.

It is just the same for you. You know the debt numbers and you want to clear the debt. To your creditor you are simply a debtor. The larger the organization that you are dealing with, the less significance your account represents among all the others. So, to stand out you need to adopt a repayment program that you know you can stick with. Own the debt and act accordingly.

The ownership in the examples with Waldo, myself and Marinela is strongly tied in with the process of reaching an agreement with a creditor and then making sure that you honor your promise to them.

ACKNOWLEDGE YOUR RESPONSIBILITY.

The other significant way that I encourage you to look at ownership of your debt is through the psychological aspect of accepting that you created it. You only have debt because of transactions you made, of agreements you gave to a certain purchase or an amount that you borrowed from someone. Your name is on the bill.

Part of owning your debt is about acknowledging that you have debted, you have taken on debt as a result of your actions.

Debt is completely neutral, just as money is. Debt takes no side. Debt has no friends nor enemies. Debt is simply the recorded liability to repay another person or organization. It is no more or less than this.

CONNECT WITH ALL OF THIS.

How do you 'take ownership' of this situation in your mind? Well, you can picture it as a massive burden on your shoulders, virtually impossible to move freely with it holding you back. You could view it as a motivator to get you into action, causing you to take positive steps forward into the process of working towards solutions. Such motivation towards what you want or away from what you either dislike or fear, is very powerful. So, a significant part of taking 'ownership' of your debt situation is around the way you look at the debt that you have. By acknowledging the extent of the debt, can you face your mental demons and fight towards the settling of the debt? Or might it be the case that the shape and weight of the debt is enough to make you give in, to collapse before it? Can the awareness of these two perspectives help you to decide how you deal with your debts? Either way you want rid of the debt burden, but you can achieve the outcome through being very clear on the way you tackle it.

From your declared motivation to be debt free, set

out an action plan or a route map of the way you seek to do this.

You've got pen and paper, haven't you? Or you might like to use a screen and a keyboard instead. Grab some quiet or private space and write about what is happening in your head as you deal with all the debt paperwork and the phone calls.

There will be boring and uninteresting static debts like the utility bills. But within your 'Money Owed' binder will be some financial results of good things you bought or trips you went on and there are positive memories and images associated with these. Yes, you may well be paying for a holiday two years after you put the tickets or hotel nights on a credit card you no longer have, but what a great trip it was!

In your amounts owed to friends and family are some stories or conversations you will long remember. Use your journal, or diary notes to put down some of your own thoughts and feelings about what is happening for you in all of this. You are attached practically and emotionally to the numbers, statements, and invoices that they appear as.

If you can hold in your mind some sense of the good things that have come to you and into your life from elements of the spending that is now recorded in your 'Money Owed' binder, then you are able to get the connection with something that is worth clearing down. I am not exactly saying that you should be grateful for the debt, but rather that if you find the good in what you had from the purchase or the loan, you can accept that you received something positive that you are now paying off in full and with an appreciation of how you benefitted.

You might need to get yourself a journal that is used only for this 'stuff' that turns up in your head each time you sit down and deal with debt paperwork and calls to your creditors. Use this journal to get such thoughts out of your head and to give yourself more space for living life in the moment, by parking much of your debt distraction in one place. You don't need to carry all of the debt arrears around in your head.

TELL IT LIKE IT IS.

So far, you know your numbers to the nearest dollar, and you can identify all the creditors. You know your current income and you also have a detailed understanding of your living expenses and monthly costs. From this understanding of what you have left you can make very specific repayment offers to your creditors and precisely because you 'own' your numbers, you can also be in a position to communicate this clearly to your creditors. The strength of your position might come across to your creditor something like this, *"I may owe you $800 but I am telling you I will make a regular weekly payment of $8 until the debt is clear. You may not want to accept this as a two year repayment program, but this is what I am starting with."* This might sound brutal and frank, yet it is the truth and so this is what you need to tell them.

Or it could sound like this, "I borrowed $2,400 from you and need to repay it. I have $400 I can give you now and based on my earnings remaining the same I can then make ten monthly payments of $200 to you until the debt is cleared."

To some extent the numbers don't matter. What counts most is your resolve to deal with the debt.

TAKE STRENGTH FROM BEING CLEAR.

Debt can fuel so much poor mental health. It can lead to stress in relationships. The potential worry it generates can drag you down and cause you to become immobilized by its weight. You need to fight this with real intention and decide not to let it have such power over you.

The collection team or the finance officer you speak with about your own debt with them will spend a huge amount of time dealing with debtors who scream or shout, who deny their liability and who communicate only in an aggressive way. Being on the receiving end of such verbal abuse and anger is difficult for a collection officer.

When you speak clearly about your debt situation, without self-pity, and with an element of gentle self-confidence, then people will hear this in your voice. From the tone of your letters, emails and phone conversations they will know they are dealing with someone who is committed to dealing with the debt. The benefit you get from 'owning the debt' psychologically is immense and will give you an additional edge when communicating with your creditors.

Your debt is something to work through, to clear off

in affordable payments. Each repayment you make is taking you closer to the place of debt freedom.

LEARNING **Points**

> This debt belongs to you.

> Only offer the repayment schedule you can afford.

> Your name is on the bill.

> Debt takes no side.

> Use a journal to log and record your thoughts and feelings.

> Communicate with your creditors based on knowing the detail.

> Make a repayment agreement and honor your promises.

THIRTEEN

You're out of the woods now

AS A CHILD GROWING up in a village, I remember that my friends and I enjoyed exploring the countryside at every opportunity. The freedom to roam where we wanted at weekends and in the summer holidays gave us the scope to wander down footpaths and green lanes by the river, or to go up into the woodland on the hilltops that overlooked the whole valley. These woods held dark mysteries that were easy and available in daylight, but always seemed less comfortable at dusk. We were always glad to get out of the woods at the end of the day and to be heading back to the comfort and safety of our homes. And so it is with you now.

HABIT TRACKING.

You have been facing your dark numbers. You have done this by first calculating and then admitting to the amounts of debt that you have. You have started tracking your expenditure. You are making notes of your contact with creditors and have begun to journal in private about your feelings associated with this debt recovery journey. You are taking control of your finances and clearing the debts one simple payment at a time.

You are making good progress and you can sense the momentum that you have created this far. You are seeing the steady reduction of your debts and you can feel the benefits of dealing with them. Congratulations on all these shifts and changes.

You are truly out of the woods, stepping into the safer place of open pathways that you choose for yourself. Your continued momentum in this good direction depends on some simple actions that you start today and continue to repeat from here on. You will become these new habits that you have been trying out and also the ones that you repeat because you know they are working for you.

S.T.O.P THE DEBTING.

See where you are.

Talk about your situation.

Occupy yourself with activities you love.

People are your support.

THIS IS A SIMPLE ACRONYM, and one that has helped me so much over the years that I spent in recovery from my debts, and later from my bankruptcy. The S.T.O.P the debting approach served my climb through the empty years when I needed to remind myself that I could create my own financial bounce back. Easy to remember and equally simple to share with other people in their own debt recovery journey.

SEE WHERE YOU ARE.

This is about taking time to look clearly at your numbers and at the debt figures in detail. It is equally about creating a regular time when you can take stock of the place you are in. Don't overdo this. Nothing at all is achieved by your obsessing about the numbers several times a day. Find your own timetable.

For me the **Weekly Review** is enough. Every Friday I look at my numbers in detail. For years I have always made my payments only on a Friday. A long time ago it was on a Friday night when getting home from work and after getting my pay that day. Then it was a Friday morning before I started an afternoon shift. I have kept to this Friday pattern of looking at my numbers over the years and know that I can open any amount of post once a week, file things, throw away unneeded documents and record my main numbers just once a week. This is more than enough to keep me on track. This perspective helps me to see the progress and keeps me clear on the situation. I can see my numbers in detail.

Remember, this is not only about paying down your debts until they are gone. It is crucial that you can set money aside into a savings account and into investments that will look after your long-term interests and aspirations. If you are paying a few bills this month, make sure that you put money aside to work for you at the same time. Incentivize yourself. The whole point about seeing where you are financially is to give yourself the perspective that things are moving consistently in the right direction, moving towards your freedom from debt.

TALK ABOUT YOUR SITUATION.

Talking is good for the soul. Even I've found this as an introvert who is happy with his own company for half of each day.

A problem shared is a problem reduced, even if it is not really a problem halved! That's the key behind this principle. When you talk with people about your debt you are allowing yourself the opportunity to gain another perspective, to have someone listen to you about what is troubling you. Another pair of ears can bring a new perspective, and possible a new solution, to something you are struggling with. This freedom of discussion can help the other person just as much as you. It might be the case that they have not been able to talk about their debt before, not known who to ask for help or some direction. By including others, in your consideration of and thoughts about your money matters, you might just be giving a lifeline to someone who is still where you have been. This person will benefit from hearing about your own personal money journey.

This conversation also affirms that you are taking action, making forward steps, reducing the debt, and talking with your creditors. It serves to remind you of your own forward direction. and can often clarify your thinking.

In the act of talking and of sharing your thoughts with another person, you are able to ask for help, and to find workable solutions. Keep talking and continue to communicate about your resolve to be free of the debt.

OCCUPY **Yourself with Activities you Love.**

As a debtor who was stuck in a helpless place, where being debt free seemed like an impossible outcome, I know how easy it is to lose sight of the life that you had actually enjoyed before the arrival of the fear and the overwhelm.

So what do you love? Are you a walker, a cyclist, rock climber? Do you love the cinema, the museums, the coffee shops, or exploring the urban landscape? Are you a gamer, an artist, an enthusiastic sketcher or maker of music?

Do you get a thrill from having friends over for a shared meal, for a social quiz session, or from catching up with people at an exhibition of new art or at an open-mike night?

The chances are high that a lot of the hobbies and activities that make you who you are have been left behind, neglected or abandoned in the face of the debt worries that have dragged you down.

Get your diary out and schedule time for yourself to do some of the things that you love. Make a date with yourself to put some pleasure and passion back in your life. Reclaim some of your hobbies. Keep doing this until you realize quite what you have been missing out on. Get back to being yourself. We all need you to be you.

PEOPLE WILL SUPPORT YOU.

You are a real gift to the world, but you need to let us in. By getting stuck in your debt troubles there is no doubt that you will have been secretive, angry, stubborn, anti-social and maybe even difficult company. Imagine that!

So, take time to spend precious moments, as well as all the completely mundane ones, with the people you have neglected along the way. Trust me here, everyone will get some benefit from this.

I once borrowed money from my brother and for the eighteen months that it remained unpaid, I felt awkward around him. I avoided meeting him. I felt such embarrassment at the situation. All of this was in my head and not in his. I wasted opportunities because of the mind games that my head was playing with me. He loves me and was confused by my awkwardness around him.

Are you missing time with someone? Is it because of embarrassment about your circumstances being different from how they used to be, or perhaps because you feel 'out of sorts' about money matters?

Are there friends you have slipped out of contact with because you feel awkward about your place in life?

Here's the thing for you to 'get'. Your friends, your family members and other people in your community or neighborhood care about you. They want to connect with you. They don't want you to pretend to be someone else, or to hide your troubles from them.

You don't have to spend money to be with a person you care about. You can see them at home and simply have a catch up with them over a cup of coffee together. You can meet them for a walk and a chat for a half hour. You can spend time with them on a bike ride or have a simple phone call together.

They have missed you while you put yourself in a self-imposed debt exile. Pick up the phone. Send a text or an email. Write a postcard. Get in touch and get together. Get out there and start to knock on a few front doors. They are waiting to hear from you. They want you to be available again.

SO I HOPE that this very straight forward S.T.O.P approach has given you some perspective on getting back to who you used to be before the debt got in the way of your happiness and fulfillment.

HEY! **Your Shower is Leaking!**

Of course, it's not really, you know that. I want this section to be a gentle reminder that the financial budgeting that we talked of at the start of the book is as important now that you are actively Climbing Out of Debt, as it was when you were feeling lost and over-whelmed.

Part of the monitoring of your Income and your Spending Record was to get you to the place where you can see a surplus build up. We all get unexpected bills and the surprise of a cost that pops up to get us. So, let's be in a place where we can always cope well with these, not by accident but instead by planning for it to happen. A plumbing leak with your shower. Some worn tires on the car, or a large utility bill in extreme cold weather. Any one of these can be a shock, but the key thing is that it should not have the power to knock you sideways.

So, make sure that you have a contingency fund to cope with this. Just yesterday I needed $640 for a bill that came out of the blue. I had to settle it by the end of the day so walked into town with the passbook account that I keep for such occasions. I drew the cash from the saving society and paid the cash to the contractor at 7pm. All dealt with in the same day.

I like to use a **Passbook Account** so that I have to physically walk into a saving society branch office to access the money. In this way I cannot impulsively get it and spend it. I like the sense that using a few different accounts like these slows down the rate at which money passes through my hands. The money is always there in case I need it.

I have different accounts like these for the categories of :

Cash Contingency

Retirement

Gifts & Treats

Holidays & Travel

Investment

The contractor was paid the $640 that drew easily from my Cash Contingency account. Knowing the money is always there gives me the peace of mind that nowadays I can cope with the unexpected. It also seems to make it easy for me to transfer some money into each account each week and I do this during that session each week (on a Friday for me) where I give some focus and attention to my money matters.

Create your own accounts for contingencies. Have some fun with finding ways that you can set up such accounts, setting aside the money each week to grow your balances in these accounts. If you have to start with $1 a week into each account, that is fine. Over time the balances will grow to $100, to $500 and to $1,000. You will enjoy seeing the accumulation of the various saving accounts. The simple act of opening them and putting money into each one from your monthly or weekly income will see the balances rise to the point where you can always sort out a future problem by throwing some of your 'set aside' money at it.

IS IT RAINING RIGHT NOW?

Should you be saving for what is often called "A Rainy Day?' I don't think so.

If you have debts right now, then your focus and your priority should be to get those debts paid off. So by all means save or set some money aside for specific things that enhance your life (for example along the lines of themes that we mentioned earlier under the idea of monies set aside for events like holidays & travel or for gifts & treats).

But a rainy day is vague. You will have a cash

account that is separate from your day to day bank account where your salary or wage goes. It's a good idea to take a portion of your regular earnings and placing this in a variety of accounts according to the themes that you want to fund. You might have to start with a percentage of your monies available after covering your debts and living expenses, but you will only be able to do it as you service the debts first. Build the contingency accounts, for these will serve you better than any rainy-day fund.

By the way, it's sunny outside now. The sky is forever blue behind any temporary clouds.

LEARNING POINTS.

> Find your own timetable for a weekly review of your money.

> Talk about your debt and repayment schedule with a trusted friend.

> Start to put personal time in the diary for you and your own well-being.

> Let good friends back in to your life and enjoy their company.

> You can always have enough to cover surprise bills.

> Building a contingency fund while clearing debts is you being practical.

> Pay yourself first by saving a fixed percentage of your regular earnings.

FOURTEEN

You can be debt free faster

EVERYTHING up to this page has been based on the assumption that you have one job or one fixed income. As we have gone through the book, I have talked about you having a job. It's a simple matter to look at your fixed income each month and to play with the expenses and then see that you have something left over for debt reduction. This is a black and white, binary kind of deal where you have a Total and you subtract the Expenses to give you a Balance for the debt.

Sure, for a lot of people this is their life and they accept the limited scope they have for anything other than spending several years in the debt repayment program with their creditors, whether this is two people they owe or twenty. There's nothing wrong with this approach. It just doesn't give you any flexibility. It's a slow, boring and endlessly repetitive route to debt freedom. The obvious upside of adopting this as the only game in town is that it is very easy to determine the date you will become debt free.

Do you like the idea of bringing forward that debt freedom date? Would it appeal to you to be able to throw money at your creditors faster, save harder and to take stronger control of the situation? No surprise here for what your response might be to these questions.

INCREASE YOUR INCOME.

Easier said than done? Not necessarily. We've already mentioned before getting here that clearing out your clutter from home could well bring in many hundreds and possibly thousands of dollars or pounds to you. You can sell off things you no longer need or which you have not used for ages and use the money to both pay down some of your debt, and put money into a savings account.

You might be working full-time for one organization. Perhaps you hustle two different jobs that create your total income for the month. With a bit of variation your money coming in is pretty much the same from one month to the next. Let's not count some occasional over-time when you look into the figures, because you can't rely on it as a consistent income.

WELCOME TO THE GIG ECONOMY!

Find yourself a decent side hustle. These days its commonly accepted that you will do what you can to generate money outside of your main job income. Look at Uber and how people can use an app on their phone to let passengers book them to become a driver. How about AirBnB as a network for generating money from that empty room you have in your apartment. The company makes it simple for you to open an account, upload a selection of photos to show off the available bedroom and your home space. They handle the verification of the guest, process payment and you get to meet a range of people while being paid additional money for an otherwise unused space in your home. Last year we received over $9,000 through the AirBnB app. Guests stayed with us just one night or a whole month. One guest stayed eleven weeks! We met people and made some new friends from Germany, the USA, Argentina, France, Spain, Poland, Zimbabwe and plenty of UK travelers too!

Online platforms allow you to sell jewelry, rent out photo images, trade vintage clothing and a thousand other things. Each one of them is a route to generating fresh money.

You can make money buying and selling items online. The web exists to allow you to find products you like or products that people buy and want. You can create a good income writing testimonials and posting these. You can blog about your passions and will be offered products to test and review. The fact you receive these for free means your work or job income allows you to further reduce your debt load. Look online at videos where people with part time web sales businesses show you how they start, what progress they make and the lessons they are learning along the way. There is no need for you to flounder all the way through on your own when there are so many online resources for you to learn from. Become hungry for new information and filter out what you don't need along the way to making money online.

NET WORK TO **build Your Net Worth.**

You can join a networking business to find and sell or distribute products you like and enjoy anyway. In our house we have two great side hustles. Find something that offers a product or product range you can enjoy for yourself and which is easy to talk about. There are so many good networking business opportunities out there. Take time to find one and make it work by working in it.

But also make sure that you 'work on' the business, meaning that you focus on the things that generate sales and the growth of your group, on the activities where you train yourself and your distributors to become better people in the process of growing the actual business. A networking business or a social marketing business is a great opportunity to have a slice of something that works well. You get the advantage of time leverage by finding and working alongside other self-motivated people, helping them to achieve their goals.

VALUE YOUR SKILLS AND TALENTS.

You can sell your time and your skills to those who want them. Can you write well? Could you explain mathematics or the principles of chemistry to a student needing help and tuition to reach or enhance their current school grades? How about your skill in a second language and sharing this in one to one or small group teaching sessions? Can you play a guitar or a piano and charge for lessons? Are you able to share your passion for woodworking, map reading, knitting, or making delicious cakes?

While many of these activities are perfect for your local community you can also develop an online support service where you provide the exact same skills through the camera on your phone, laptop or desktop. Others log in and watch and learn. You can sell this service on a one to one individual basis or you can record your eating and sell it to multiple clients. You could have three clients visiting you at home for an hour each week and bring in an extra $100 for this activity. Or you could have twenty people subscribing to a weekly online video call or recorded learning session and generate several hundred dollars each week in this manner. The main thing is that they pay you for your time or for your recorded skill set and you get to bank the money.

MAKE **Money Doing what you Love.**

> The easiest way to find additional income is to make a list of your favorite hobbies,

passions and activities.

> Now highlight the activities that you would be happy receiving money for.

> Finally, select the absolute favorite one and think of ten ways you could sell, offer,

or provide a service to other people in providing this to others.

> Practice that offer or make those sales until you have received your first $100.

> Repeat to get to $500 and then to $1,000.

You now have a business that you can continue to generate money with. As simple as this process may seem to be, it is a great way to get intuitively and quickly to a place where you can enjoy making money.

PAY Down the Debt or Save some Money?

For me it has always felt right to split whatever extra money I brought in and spread it equally across debt reduction and into savings accounts. I tried for more than a year to only throw the extra money at debt reduction, but I could not find any emotional satisfaction in only seeing the debt reduce. We are all different and will look at the debt issue in ways that are unique to ourselves. Find what is right for yourself and focus on enjoying the whole journey.

CELEBRATE YOUR RESULTS.

It is not just about getting to the place where all your debt is gone and realizing with shock that you are free of debt but have no available cash funds. For many of us that is a hollow victory.

Freedom from debt might be a very good place to reach after two or three years and in that time scale you will certainly need some encouragement. You may find it helpful to reward yourself by setting debt reduction goals and celebrate these. For example, if you owe

$1,500 to a creditor break this down into perhaps 15 amounts of $100. Use a paper chart and color in a section of a scaled version of the $1,500 debt.

Every time you pay down $100 is a great moment but reducing each unit of $500 is cause for even bigger celebration. Make the achievement of the debt reduction something you treat yourself to. It can be time doing something you love, or a simple treat out at a coffee shop, a day out for a hobby with friends. Don't neglect yourself in the hard work of becoming debt free. You must look after yourself along the way.

When you have an extra $100 and you have already made your prearranged debt repayment commitments for that week or month, stop to think about what you might do with the $100 left over. You could throw it perhaps at your highest percentage debt account or you could put it towards clearing one of the smallest debt balances. Both would feel good. Consider a different approach. Put half of that amount (in this case we are talking about $50) into a savings account. This could be online or in a physical passbook that you take into a bank or savings branch for them to credit your account. Build up a savings buffer with every opportunity that you can. Aim for $500 and then grow the savings to $1,000 with one bank or savings society.

You may only get 1% or 2% interest but that is far less important than you seeing the steady buildup of some savings. We used to refer to this as 'rainy day' money when I was a young adult. I guess it was something to do with having money for when you needed to make house repairs after damage caused by severe weather. Perhaps it goes back to the days of agricultural about when often there was no paid work on a 'rainy day'. But bad stuff will happen, and surprises will come in the form of unexpected bills. So, having a side account which is purely for accumulating spare money is a very important thing for you to work upon. When you sell some of the clutter in your house the proceeds could go in here. If you have a yard sale or start trawling shops for things which are being sold below true value and you then sell these online for a profit, this is the account where you will place the proceeds of each trade.

Once you have reached this significant $1,000 amount with one account start another and build to another $1,000. There are a few reasons why you should build to another $1,000 with a different bank or savings company. Your credit rating has been damaged over the years and you want to grow the rating back to a healthier status. Having good balances in different institutions will go some way to helping this credit scoring process. The other reason is that having the money in different places means it will take longer for you to draw out the money and reduce your temptation to spending it. You will feel your confidence and belief grow along with your savings. You are still paying down your debt and maintaining regular correspondence with your creditors but now you are building some financial strength for yourself other than seeing everything going to debt repayment.

It might seem too difficult to arrive at an account with $1,000 in it but start this week by putting aside $10 or $20. Then keep repeating the process. You can physically walk some cash into a savings bank branch. You can do a regular online transfer. I have an app on my phone which takes the unused pennies from each card transaction and pushes it into a savings account. So, for a $3.65 spend on my card the app will transfer 35c into the savings account. Talk about an easy way to see your savings grow.

PEER TO PEER LENDING OPPORTUNITIES.

Once you have built up a couple or more buffer accounts with $1,000 or $1,000 in then you can consider getting better returns on your spare funds. You are continuing to pay down debt month on month and should now be in a position where you are earning money and rebuilding your credit position for the future. For example, you might want to buy a house in the coming years, set up a new business with physical or digital assets, or simply to change banks and have a decent credit history when this time comes.

THERE ARE numerous peer to peer (or people to people) lending groups online where returns of 5% to 9% are steadily achieved. A peer to peer lender exists online and receives deposits from those who seek to lend and then apportions out what they deposit to different lenders. For example, you might place $500 into such a lending platform. Different lenders require a variety of starting balances but $100 seems quite common. After you have deposited this sort of figure you can add smaller amounts whenever you choose. I use three different lending platforms and transfer spare money into each account each week. It can be $25 or $10 as a minimum each week. They don't mind.

As your account balance grows, they will lend the money out to their borrowers. They won't lend that money to one person but will instead take that $500 and divide it so that you are lending $10 to 50 different people seeking to borrow. They do exactly the same with all other lenders and so each of you only has a limited (in this case $10) exposure to any one borrower. The lending platform will give you the option to select the risk profile you want to have when lending and will offer you higher returns to where you allocate money into loans to people with a higher risk calculation attached to their profile. You can choose a return that you are comfortable with based on your approach to risk.

CUT YOUR COSTS!

It's all well and good to boost your income and maintain the same lifestyle. This can work but might simply mean that you take longer to be free of your debt. To get rid of your debt as fast as possible you will need to do both - Increase your income and Cut your costs.

This is radical and very often seems to be ignored by a lot of people when considering the scope to become free of debt. Many pundits think that you should not change your lifestyle to become debt free and I disagree with them on this. You don't have to, but you might be carrying debt for several years more than you need to if you are not willing to at least try to find new ways to get debt free faster! This is why I have saved it to the last in this particular chapter.

EXAMPLE 1.

I have cleared debt fast before by moving from a four-bed house on my own to sharing a three-bed house with a friend. My household expenses went down by $400 a month and the $4,800 this saved me allowed me to clear three debts that totaled $4,000 in just over ten months. It was a real win - win situation to do this. It was fun finding a new area and a less expensive rental opportunity that I could share with a friend.

EXAMPLE 2.

There was a time when I was driving just under 110 miles every day in my round trip to work and back, so about 550 - 600 miles each working week. The driving took about three hours of my day but also cost me a load of money in fuel, tires and depreciation on the car. A change in my home situation meant that it was worth considering a new job closer to home. I found a decent job one mile from home and could walk there in any weather. Not only did I then find myself in a place where I was saving more than fifteen hours a week, but I was also saving close on $500 each month on fuel. Was I better off with an extra 60 hours a month and $6,000 that stayed in my bank account? Absolutely.

So, let's look at you and your circumstances and see what you can find in terms of money saved by cutting your costs at home.

Let's say you have an amount of $10,000 of debt. By now you know that this is just a model of your actual debt and we use this to help you focus on finding a solution to clear the debt.

Set a goal. How can you find $10,000 worth of savings to eradicate the debt of that same value?

HERE ARE some examples for you to think about and use to stimulate your own ideas.

> Could you cut your accommodation costs by $5,000 per year for two years and be debt free?

> How about reducing your household food bill by $100 per month over 100 months to be debt free?

> Might you be able to get a lesser value car finance package to save $50 or $100 each month?

> If you are incurring car fuel costs of $500 per month just to travel to and from work, what could you do with the savings if you moved closer to work, found a new job closer to home, used cheaper public transport instead of using the car so often, throwing the savings at the $10,000 debt figure?

> What about identifying how many rooms in your house are the equivalent of the clutter you have at home, then downsizing by that value? This way you sell the junk or unused items for perhaps $2,000 which goes into savings or debt reduction, but you move to a property that is quite good enough but which saves you $200

a month on rent or mortgage costs and reduces your city tax at the same time.

In any of these examples – each designed to get you thinking more creatively about debt reduction and total debt freedom – you connect with the debt figure you want to clear and look at simple act that reduce your monthly costs in a completely predictable and clear way.

Good luck with coming up with ways to reduce costs and throw money at the debt until you are free.

LEARNING POINTS.

> Find yourself a decent side hustle and boost your income.

> Leverage your time and money by helping others to achieve.

> Take an item or service you like and practice selling for a profit.

> You can sell anything via goo online auction and sales platforms.

> Build a financial buffer for confidence and to create practical financial strength.

> It's OK to be repaying debts while you still have good savings.

> Consider the option to lend or invest to create a profit.

FIFTEEN

Moving on, moving forward

YOU NOW HAVE structures and simple systems in place to help you clear your debts. You have negotiated payments with your creditors and have begun the steady process of making regular repayments. Hopefully you are feeling the real benefits of less fear, of knowing that you are back in control again, and can embrace the greater happiness of standing on your own feet again financially.

Making your payments again and on a regular basis, gives you the confidence that the debt is reducing each week. You are clearing head space to let in greater joy, feelings of relief and that sense of being in a new and better place emotionally. You need to acknowledge this, to immerse yourself in the celebration of what you have accomplished. Congratulations on having made a bold change in your behavior. This will create absolutely the most liberating shift towards your own financial free-dom, giving you the ability to start choosing how you lead your life from here on.

You might have reached this page on the first read of this book and before you have put some or many of the ideas here into practice. Possibly you have read a few chapters, acted on them and put the book aside for a few months as you have structured your debt free program and just decided to finish the book. My hope is that you have got to this chapter after at least putting into a place a budget, establishing a regular debt Repayment Figure and after Communicating with your creditors.

With this being the case, you just need to remind yourself to stick with the program, to keep yourself on track with the progress that you have started. Here are some ideas to help you.

AVOID THE TEMPTATION TO DEBT.

I can't tell you to stop reading magazines, to close your eyes to adverts on roadside billboards, or on metro posters. I don't want to be so foolish! Every day you are bombarded with messages and images that encourage you to:

"Buy this Sofa now (and pay for it in 24 months)."

"Enjoy a Holiday with us next year (and pay just $100 deposit today)."

"Join our Cinema group and enjoy unlimited films (with a regular $30 monthly payment)."

"Drive away this gorgeous Car for just $256 a month (and an $8,000 early deposit payment today)."

According to the advertisers and the marketing departments you really can have what you want. You just have to pay for it later, and the years of debt commitments will all be explained in that small print which the salespeople tend not to focus on.

You know enough already that you can set aside money within your budget – and alongside your debt freedom payments – to save up cash for a short break holiday; that you can buy an older model car for cash when the depreciation and fall in value has already happened; that you can find a stylish sofa in a thrift store or charity shop for just a fraction of its new "on finance" price; that you can get an online film subscription for pennies and enjoy so many movies.

Avoid the temptation to overspend and make sure that you stay away from 'easy' borrowing. When an offer is really compelling for you find a way to get the same or similar benefits within your real budget, rather than stretching yourself when it is just not necessary or required.

When tempted to debt you need to ask yourself some basic questions:

Do I need this?

Does it add great value to my life?

Is the cost of acquiring this item worth the delay in me making other repayments?

STAY CLOSE TO GOOD FRIENDS.

In the course of getting to grips with the materials in this book you will have already found a few good people who know your situation. They may be from existing family and friends, could be newly met people, or perhaps members of a Money Discussion Group or a Debt Action meeting that you attend.

You can pick up the phone and talk with someone who will understand when you say that you've been tempted by something you can't afford, or that you are getting impatient with the slow, steady repayments of your debt.

This person will understand, will give you some friendly counsel and will keep you on track. You know you can do it yourself, but it's good to be able to talk through things when you feel a bit weak.

Staying accountable to a friend who knows the debt journey you are going through and the progress you have committed to, this is a valuable relationship. Take advantage of the opportunity you have to report how you feel over your money, about your spending behaviors and at those times when you are tempted toward debt action, call them and share with them how you are feeling. Rather than only use that support when you feel in danger of over spending, make a regular time at least once each month to talk with them about your finances, your cash flow and the situation of your various debts and the prepayments you are making towards them. Be just as accountable to them as they expect you to be accountable and responsible yourself.

Consider creating a money support group where you meet up once a month with a few people to talk about experience of climbing out of debt. Each time you get together, whether in a living room, community hall or coffee shop, you can discuss the progress you are making. Track the actual amount you have repaid.

Monitor the value of this figure as a percentage of the total debt. Share different letter templates to see how you are communicating with creditors and earning their respect for your approach to debt reduction.

Talk about the impact of your repayments on a credit score or how you have settled into regular repayment. Share about the benefits of building a savings pot of $250 and then $500 and on to $1,000 for different themed activities such as a holiday, gifts and treats, a retirement fund.

You will have a tremendous time doing this with a small group, encouraging and helping one another as you each share the discoveries and results since the previous gathering.

BE AN OBSERVER AND A SUPPORTER.

You have made great progress towards first recognizing your debt problem and then dealing with each debt and creditor responsibly. Think back to how things were when you felt alone with your debt and unsure of where to turn for help and to discuss the challenges you were facing. With the different position you are in now, do you think you might be able to act in support of someone who is struggling each day with the weight of their debts? Keep a watchful eye out for those in your own social and work circles who might be getting into financial difficulty.

Listen for complaints about struggling with unexpected bills, or for comments about being at the limit of a bank overdraft or at the bad end of a credit card limit.

Is someone dropping out of social events for fear of not being able to manage the $20? Has a friend gone to ground over their money worries about a $200 bill they cannot deal with?

Be a supporter to them. You do this by sharing the knowledge that you are picking up, by talking with them about what is working for you in all of this. Tools that have been useful and helpful to you will very likely be well received by them. Can you steer them towards a money support group or an online network? You have templates for income & expenditure and for letters to send to creditors. Feel free and able to help this person with what you have learned along the journey.

BE GRATEFUL.

Notice how far you have come by taking time to look around your home at the rooms where you once nervously accumulated bags or boxes of debt paperwork, unopened post and where you hid from the reality of your debts. Can you recall the emotions you felt when things were out of control? Think back to the fear and the anxiety you carried with you when you were ignoring acting on the debts.

STAY ORGANIZED.

See how much things have changed in your physical living space since you took action against the debt. What happened to the chaos of debt paperwork spread around the house, some of it hidden and placed out of sight. Why did you do this? Was it out of fear, shame and embarrassment at the scale of what seemed like total overwhelm? Now you have the benefit of knowing that your money files are well organized. You can open them at any time to see reducing balances and specific timetables for becoming free of your debt.

The difference between where you were before with the lack of order and the place you have reached today in getting rid of unwanted and unhelpful duplicate paperwork, by giving structure and order to your creditor paperwork, all of this has brought you real benefits emotionally and in terms of peace of mind. Notice the difference between the two places and resolve to stay on top of the weekly reviews, to continue filing only the paperwork and statements that you must keep and getting rid of everything else.

You are now organized for debt reduction alongside for the growth of your savings. You are managing home organization to include all financial paperwork and you know where to find the letters, statements or payment records whenever you need to refer to them.

How does it make you feel to know that you have come this far? I am sure that you are in a far better place now and that you will continue to enjoy actively managing your debts down and watching your savings grow.

CONGRATULATIONS to you for your commitment to this achievement and to being honest with yourself about what will be required as you manage the process of becoming free of debt and in control of your finances.

Enjoy the money journey and take it just one day at a time.

Nick

Yorkshire, England

LEARNING POINTS.

> Manage your paperwork systems to master steady repayment.

> You have structured your own Debt Free program.

> Enjoy the pleasure of buying with cash.

> Find an Accountability Partner for discussing your debt reduction steps.

> Consider starting your own Money Support Group.

> Listen out for those needing personal help in facing their debts.

> Notice your feelings as you see your debts reduce.

> Stay grounded in today and be grateful for all that you have and do.

About the Author

Collector of books, fan of new reading and ever fascinated with the power of the written world to bring new ideas and thinking.

As an author I love time spent at my desk in my dedicated writing shed at the bottom of the garden or at a table in a neighbourhood coffee shop. I love to be with pens and paper working through ideas for a manuscript or a presentation.

Best of all is getting a concept out of my head and into a conversation with a reader, discussing our different ways of approaching something which unites all of us. This could be around Financial Thinking and Personal Budgeting, dealing with the Clutter we accumulate in our living spaces or wanting solutions and new ways of thinking about Debt so that we can enjoy more control of our money on the way to financial peace of mind.

It is so great to do what I enjoy with the writing, getting good feedback for the books that people enjoy and which can be seen to be making a positive difference.

Find Nick at www.nicksturgeonbooks.com

Printed in Great Britain
by Amazon

24023851R00108

How do you feel about your debt?

Do you feel guilty that you got yourself into your current situation? Do you lay awake worrying about how you're going to pay the next bill to land on your doormat, dreading the next heavy knock on the door?

It's time to leave this guilt and fear behind. It's time to take action to manage your debts and get them under control so you can live your life again.

Nick Sturgeon has been on both sides of debt: successful entrepreneur and property owner, he lost almost everything and was forced to rebuild his life while burdened by historical debt.

To do this, he created a step by step approach for getting control of your debt. He has since used this approach and method in his role as a money advice worker to help people achieve greater financial control and freedom from money worry.

You can use these same steps to help yourself with **Climbing Out of Debt.**

ISBN 9781838130404

9 781838 130404

www.nicksturgeonbooks.com